Monuments and Main Streets

Monuments and Main Streets
Messages from Architecture

Harris Stone

Monthly Review Press
New York

Library of Congress Cataloging in Publication Data

Stone, Harris, 1934–
    Monuments and main streets.

    Bibliography: p.
    1. Architecture and society -- Addresses,
essays, lectures. 2. Architecture and
history -- Addresses, essays, lectures.
I Title.
NA 2543. S6 S78 1983   720'.1'03   83-42528
ISBN 0-85345-638-0
ISBN 0-85345-639-9 (pbk.)

Monthly Review Press
155 West 23rd Street, New York, N.Y. 10011

Manufactured in the United States of America

10 9 8 7 6 5 4 3 2 1

CONTENTS

INTRODUCTION. Monuments and Main Streets follows a line of investigation that touches on questions about modern architecture in relation to art, work, the machine, and nature. The generally accepted notion that industrial technology and hand craftsmanship are mutually exclusive is explicitly rejected, as is the currently fashionable notion that an authentic architecture can be based on the separation of the design from the construction process. Forward-thrusting tendencies within modern architecture are not viewed as isolated from and opposed to backward-leaning tendencies but as interacting parts of the historical process by which architecture develops. Monumental and vernacular architecture, tower and street are not studied as separate building traditions that develop independently of one another; rather, they are examined as different aspects of a common cultural heritage.

My method as an author parallels the method of an architect, standing before a sheet of paper on which the rough outline of an idea is drawn. The idea is developed in a series of sketches on sheets of tracing paper placed one on top of another over the initial drawing. Each tracing focuses on a different aspect of the idea that by a slight adjustment of the eye can be viewed independently,

7

in relation to another tracing, or as part of a sequence of tracings.

If there is a single idea underlying all the tracings for this and my previous book, Workbook of an Unsuccessful Architect, it came into focus at a particular moment. It was the late 1960's. I was a member of a small group of political activists involved in the struggles of the time: Vietnam, Civil Rights, Urban Renewal.

I was analyzing the design of a corporate headquarters building. I had been struggling with the same page all morning. Putting down my pen, I stood up and stared out the window. The idea was out of focus. The lines on the page were lifeless. I began to rummage among the discarded versions that littered the drafting table. Suddenly I stopped, gathered up all the versions, and stuffed them into the wastebasket. I could not assess my writing and drawing because of the distance between the way I was working and the way published books usually look. Typeset, photographs, layout -- I was handwriting and sketching in trying to give shape to my ideas.

I retrieved one of the pages with its rough sketches and clumsy handwriting and took it to an offset print shop run by friends from our political group. They photographed the page, made a plate, ran it off. My line work was too thick, the proportion of illustrated text to page was wrong for the paper stock, both the text and drawings needed more attention, but that page was clearly and unmistakably defined. Its essential features would not be altered, only heightened by the changes I could now foresee.

Friends from our political group who had moved to another city asked to see what I was working on. I realized that my handwritten and illustrated pages would photocopy well and at no great expense. I made a copy of the manuscript and mailed it off. They read it, were excited about it, and persuaded Monthly Review Press to consider it for publication. Intrigued by a manuscript dealing with the visual arts from a left perspective that could be printed without worrying about elaborate layout and photographic work, Monthly Review decided to publish it.

The sequence of events that resulted in the publication of Workbook of an Unsuccessful Architect enabled me to confront a number of my architectural and political concerns simultaneously and to perceive their interrelatedness. Workbook was an odd juxtaposition of material that cut across disciplinary lines and called for an investigative procedure of superimposed interpretations. Monuments and Main Streets continues the exploration begun in Workbook and goes on to pose new questions that produced a refinement of my analytic technique into a series of verbal and visual tracings.

This book begins with a two-part essay, "Messages From the Media and the Fields," that looks critically at the almost total separation of designer and builder in modern architecture. Part one, "Messages From the Media," focuses on the highly publicized work of a group of contemporary architects whose attempt to accept the separation as the defining feature of their architecture is heralded as post-modern by the architectural press. Part two, "Message From the Fields," describes the struggle of an anonymous group of people to overcome the separation in their effort to convert a small farm into a laboratory of socially appropriate building technology and design.

In the second essay, "Messages From the Past," the circular temple is traced from Stonehenge to the Guggenheim Museum as an architectural theme that has been developed in different ways in different eras.

Nostalgia for the past coupled with fantasies for the future is generally considered to be a post-modern dilemma. The masters of modern architecture are thought to have held simple and clear-cut attitudes towards both the architecture of the past (iconoclastic) and technology of the future (prophetic). The problematic relationship between the backward-leaning and forward-thrusting tendencies within

INTRODUCTION

five acknowledged masterpieces of modern architecture is examined in the third essay, "Messages of Belief."

As my study of the relationships between art and technology in the sequence of circular temples (second essay) progressed, I began to observe a combination of symbolic and practical thinking not only in the design of the monuments but also in the system of roadways that link them to one another across the ages. This observation provided the impetus for "Story of the Road," which focuses on the formation of the roadways and streets apart from the monuments. The study appears in this book as part one of the fourth essay, "Messages From Main Street."

The second part of the essay, "City Streets," searches for the significance of the modest buildings that line Main Street. Viewed independently, the components of Main Street are incoherent and inconsequential. Viewed collectively, however, they form a distinct urban idea. At the time I was studying this idea, the struggle of a group of architects, designers, and artists in Montreal against the wholesale destruction of a major downtown street for the sake of a questionable development program was making news. I viewed the news story a through a sheet of tracing paper on which the idea of Main Street had been inscribed.

This process enabled me to see and assess more clearly both the idea of Main Street and the political struggle over its design taking place in Montréal and other cities.

The composition of Monuments and Main Streets is roughly symmetrical in both form and content. Monumental buildings provide the focus of the two central essays. Monuments are important, but they constitute a small fraction of the built environment. Small buildings, modest streets, and architects at work provide the focus of the two-part essays with which the book begins and ends.

MESSAGES FROM THE MEDIA
AND THE FIELDS

PREFACE. The greeks utilized only one procedure of mechanically reproducing building components: shaping in a mold. The Roman uses of kiln firing and of concrete were important developments, but of the same procedure.

Roman arch, concrete with brick face.   Roman brick-kiln (reconstruction).

With the increasing emphasis upon mechanized rather than human or animal power that began in the Middle Ages, the large-scale reproduction of building components became possible. However, it was not until the development of the factory system at the end of the eighteenth century that the technique of reproducing architectural elements reached a new stage.

By 1840 there were carefully detailed pattern books for builders of almost

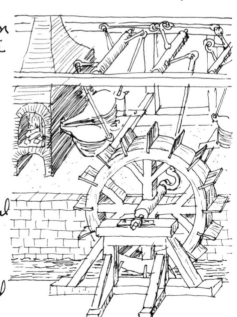

Water driven bellows (reconstruction).

every historical style and regional variation. To an ever greater degree a particular building technique or system of ornamentation came to be valued less for its uniqueness than for its reproducibility.

THE

BUILDER'S DIRECTOR,
OR
BENCH-MATE:
BEING

A POCKET-TREASURY
OF THE

Grecian, Roman, and Gothic ORDERS
of ARCHITECTURE,

Made eaſy to the meaneſt Capacity by near 500 Examples,
Improved from the beſt AUTHORS,
Ancient and Modern,

Of Pedeſtals, Baſes, Shafts, Capitals, Columns, Architraves, Freezes, Brackets, Cornices, Arches, Impoſts, Key-ſtones, Truſſes, Moldings of Raking Pediments, Frontiſpieces, Portico's, Arcades, Colonades, Chimney-Pieces, Fretts, Guilochi's, Groins, Weatherings, Moldings for Tabernacle's, Frames, &c.
PROPORTIONED
By MINUTES and by EQUAL PARTS.

The like never before Publiſhed.

Engraved on 184 Copper Plates,
WHEREIN
The Orders of ANDREA PALLADIO are truly laid down, free from erroneous Meaſures.

Written for the Uſe of Gentlemen delighting in True ARCHITECTURE; and for Maſters and Workmen to Draw from and Work after.

By BATTY LANGLEY, Architect.

LONDON: Printed for and ſold by H. PIERS, oppoſite Dean ſtreet, in High-Holborn, 1751.

In 1851 the Crystal Palace, a building of factory built, mass produced, interchangeable parts, was assembled on one site, taken apart, and reassembled elsewhere. For the first time in the history of architecture a particular building was not limited to a particular time and place. This freedom became the defining characteristic of "modern" architecture.

LONDON: Crystal Palace under construction, 1850.

"A house is a machine for living in," Le Corbusier proclaimed in defiance of the eclectic architecture of the early decades of the twentieth century. The architecture of antiquity had been heroic, the architecture of religion blessed; from now on it simply had to work.

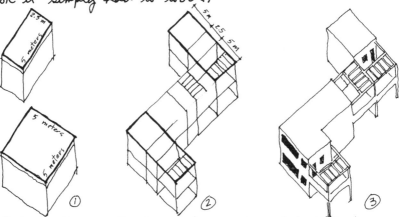

PESSAC, FRANCE: Housing, preliminary study of standardization, 1925.

PESSAC: Le Corbusier's design as built, 1926.

Architecture could be freed from eclecticism, an anachronistic system of historical ornamentation, as architects such as Le Corbusier demonstrated, but not from the historical process.

PESSAC: Le Corbusier's design as modified by residents, 1969.

By mid-century the paradox represented by equating a house with a machine was eclipsed by the contradiction between the design and the construction process. A design sketched by an architect is a carefully reasoned abstract argument; it exists in the realm of universal ideas. The actual building project, on the other hand, is thought out in terms of reinforcing bars and heating ducts. What architects call "working drawings," construction workers jokingly refer to as "the funny papers."

Louis Kahn was troubled by the fact that

PREFACE

architectural design and building construction exist in separate realms. A story is told of his concern about the discrepancy in scale between his design for a small housing project and the overpowering presence of a gigantic crane on the construction site.

The contradiction between design and construction process defines the contemporary architectural scene to such an extent that a group of architects, generally referred to as "post-modernists," have attempted to embrace the contradiction and make it central to their design process. For them, unlike Le Corbusier and Louis Kahn, architecture does not have to work. Their position and its implications are discussed in part one, "Messages From the Media."

Part two, "Message From the Field," presents a contrasting position: a small group of architects and students on a farm, away from the eye of the media, sifting through existing design and construction concepts, searching for new connections, and experimenting with alternative technologies.

SOURCES

Benjamin, Walter. "The Work of Art in the Age of Mechanical Reproduction," Illuminations. New York: Schocken Books, 1969.

Singer, Holmyard, and Hall (eds). A History of Technology. London: Oxford University Press, 1955.

PART 1-- MESSAGES FROM THE MEDIA.

FASHIONABLY AVANT-GARDE, idolized in Japan not unlike a rock star and paid accordingly, Kisho Kurokawa represents a new kind of architect: he is a media event.

"The capsule is cyborg architecture," he stated in an article written in 1969, explaining in a footnote that the word "cyborg" is "an organism which is partly automated, based on feedback and information processes that usually appears in science fiction as half man, half machine." Kurokawa's work is filled with such jarring analogies and metaphors. Some appear fairly regularly and are central to his thinking; others are used only once or twice, more as spice than as basic ingredients. Sometimes they are illuminating, at other times confusing. It does not seem to matter, for good or bad, right or wrong, these jarring

Hotel unit

Bath unit

Balcony unit

Bedroom unit

PROJECT

juxtapositions tend to be
mediagenic.

As in his design for
the Nakagin Capsule
Tower, 1972, the summer
retreat he designed for
himself the same year
is subdivided into
separate factory-built,
lightweight steel capsules
attached with high-tension
bolts to a poured-in-place
concrete service and
circulation shaft. Each
capsule is independentty
cantilevered from the
shaft so that it can
be easily removed and
replaced with newer
capsules as they are
developed. Despite
this space-age image

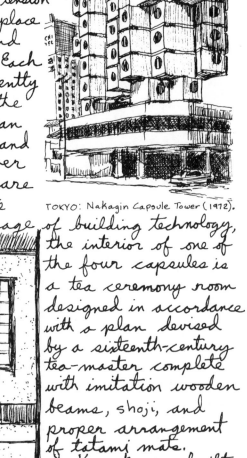

TOKYO: Nakagin Capsule Tower (1972).

of building technology,
the interior of one of
the four capsules is
a tea ceremony room
designed in accordance
with a plan devised
by a sixteenth-century
tea-master complete
with imitation wooden
beams, shoji, and
proper arrangement
of tatami mats.
Kurokawa built

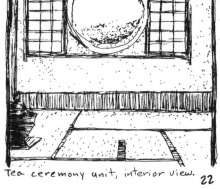

Tea ceremony unit, interior view.

his summer retreat, but "has seen it only twice in two years and then for a few moments" (Charles Jencks); more to the point, however, the design received extensive coverage in the media. Kurokawa wrote about it as follows:

> The oriental individuum is not the independent individual of the West... The tea room for the tea ceremony shows how the concept of the individuum is applied to building... from within the tiny room [the participants] can enjoy sensing the vastness of nature...
> I intended my capsule spaces to be a declaration of war in support of the restoration of oriental individuum...

Oriental individuum, tea ceremony, vastness of nature, declaration of war... the images tumble over each other abstracted from social reality, directed towards the magnifying lens of the media. No specific public response is expected other than

KARUISAWA: Capsule summer house (1972), view from below.

recognition of the architectural persona that is being created.

For the pioneers of modern architecture what might be called "publicity" or, more accurately, "propaganda" was essential. They wrote manifestos and made concerted efforts to publicize their work. For example, le Corbusier began his career editing a journal of literature and art, L'Esprit Nouveau, in which he published parts of what was to become his book, Towards a New Architecture, and for which he designed an exhibition pavilion in 1925.

Today the media are the creators of many new architectures, most of which are as disposable as any other commodity. Few architects would need to be reminded who designed the Pavillon de l'Esprit Nouveau, but many would have to be told again who

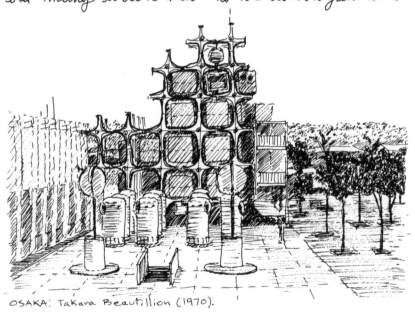

OSAKA: Takara Beautillion (1970).

designed what one critic described at the time as "the most exciting piece of architecture among the almost hysterically exciting company of buildings" at Osaka's Expo '70 -- Kurokawa's pavilion for the Takara Group of furniture companies, in which capsules for exhibition use were plugged into a three-dimensional grid of bent steel pipes to whose "empty exhibitionist extensions," as the critic noted, the designer "could not resist adding a few unuseable extra units..." (Robin Boyd).

Such a structure may appear hysterically exciting in the context of an exposition, but as a residence it raises troubling questions. Never has the notion of the house as "a machine for living in" so sorted, boxed, and delivered people up to industrial technology, or produced such a monstrous discrepancy between the design process and the elements of human existence

Takara Beautillion, exterior.

theoretically being accommodated. Worse than this, an increasing number of architects view such a discrepancy as a defining characteristic of their work.

CARDBOARD ARCHITECTURE : Peter Eisenman's House II, 1969.

"My work can be described by the term 'cardboard'," says Peter Eisenman, director of the Institute for Architecture and Urban Studies (IAUS), New York City; "it is a precise metaphor of my intentions." And so saying, he dismisses the stricture against "paper architecture", a phrase used by architects to describe a design that may be exciting on paper but does not work in reality.

"The most important thing for Eisenman," an IAUS faculty member has said, "is not the finished product itself, but the operations which gave rise to it." For Eisenman the most important thing is the design process -- that is, his own drawings and cardboard models --

not the actual building or project. He thinks of the building as something that is "in a sense, unreal" and is amused that people have mistaken photographs of the cardboard model of a house he designed with photographs of the actual building.

CARDBOARD ARCHITECTURE: designing House III, 1973.

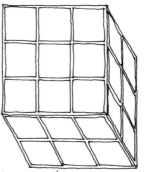

Column grid

Eisenman adopts the expedient of reasoning only about conventional architectural symbols, which as black marks on white paper are particular objects, but which by definition are universal. He even has a formula: "First, to reduce or unload the existing meaning from the elements in actual space so that the forms can be seen as a series of primitive marks [for example, the designer ignores the fact that columns are supposed to support structural loads and sees them simply as dots in space]. Second, to take these marks and structure the environment [that is, the designer proceeds to locate these

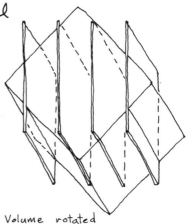

Volume rotated

Volume split

27

column/dots abitrarily].
Third, to relate this structure
to another structure of a
more abstract and
fundamental nature..."

For Eisenman truth
is something that lurks
behind or above contrary
assertions. He explains
that "layering [which is
the way the designer
attempts to relate those
arbitrarily placed
column/dots to one
another] gives order to
the base system [that
is, the arbitrarily placed
column/dots] and generates
a system of implied
spatial oppositions." Like
Eurydice, truth in this
context is something that
evaporates when it is
seen.

Underneath Eisenman's
"overlaid and interacting
structures" is an urge
to reconstruct the natural
environment on the model
of a simple machine.
He wants to "generate
more rational form,
that is, form designed
with more precise

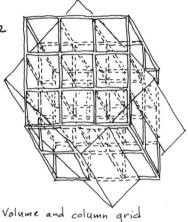

Volume and column grid

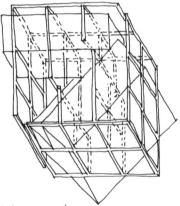

Columns and walls

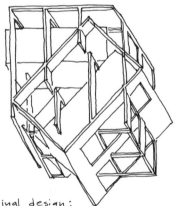

Final design:
volume, walls, and columns

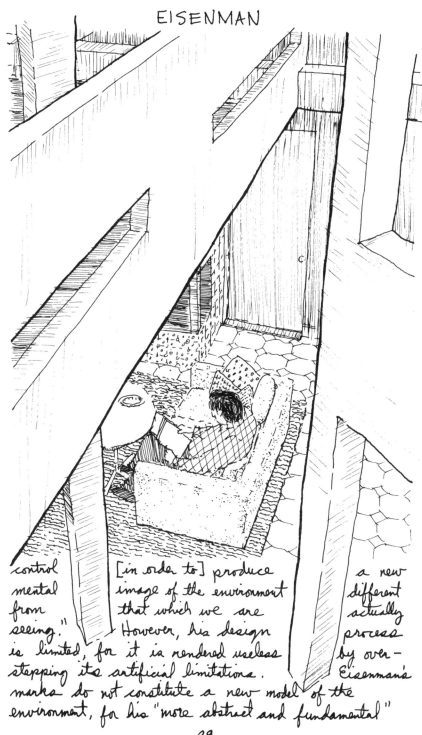

control [in order to] produce a new
mental image of the environment different
from that which we are actually
seeing." However, his design process
is limited, for it is rendered useless by over-
stepping its artificial limitations. Eisenman's
marks do not constitute a new model of the
environment, for his "more abstract and fundamental"

matrix changes from design to design. His marks do not even supply a direction -- a column/dot is a column/dot.

It is impossible to overlook the distant relationships of Eisenman's architecture with that kind of minimal art which attempts to resemble a machine without fulfilling its function and, in so doing, becomes a commentary on our society. In Eisenman's architecture the disinterest of the alienated worker becomes the law of the language of art.

CARDBOARD ARCHITECTURE: Interior, House VI, 1977.

In 1976 IAUS mounted an exhibition, "Idea as Model," which explored the notion that as Eisenman explained it, "a model of a building could be something other than a narrative record of a project or a building... that models, like architectural drawings, could well have an artistic or conceptual existence of their own, one which was relatively independent of the project they represented." And so saying, he dismissed the traditional function of the architect as a designer who devises structures for specific needs utilizing the limited number of building materials and techniques of the traditional building crafts. The point was underlined in a postscript written for the exhibition catalogue, whose publication by Rizzoli was delayed until 1981:

Four years have passed since the close of the exhibition "Idea as Model." In the interval, architecture has changed in several ways... First, models and drawings have been taken up by the galleries. Architects have stopped pretending that they are above selling their ideas as works of art... Second, and more important, the modernists have lost the war... The loss of faith in architecture has advanced so far in recent years that... only variety, uncertainty, and incompleteness will do... The only way now to deal with reality is

Grade level of Town Square

Proposed four-foot high model of House IIa.

Proposed full-scale House IIa with four-foot high model of house within.

CARDBOARD ARCHITECTURE: House IIa, 1978. Project for Cannaregio.

through the extremes of imagination...
[The postscript concluded that] history is
the issue now... The question put to
history is whether it can offer liberation...

This notion has been discussed by
other commentators using other words:
much has been written about "functional"
versus "eclectic" architecture, especially
in the opening decades of the twentieth
century, and, more recently, about
"modernist" versus "historicist" architecture.
The names given to the contending trends
have changed but not the conflict between
the dynamic, forward-thrusting and
static, backward-leaning tendencies
within architecture. The continuing nature
of the conflict suggests that it is more than
a game in which two distinct positions
are marked out and set in opposition to
each other, more than a struggle between
one group of designers who favor machine-
like imagery derived from the most advanced
forms of industrial technology and a
second group who wish to cloak their
designs with images derived from the
past. It is a conflict fought out not only
in the development of modern architecture,
but often in the course of an architect's
career, sometimes in the evolution of an
architectural design.

After Robert Venturi
wrote Complexity and
Contradiction in Architecture
(New York: Museum of

DECORATED SHED

Modern Art, 1966), he collaborated with two other members of his architectural firm, Denise Scott Brown and Stephen Izenour, in writing the book Learning from Las Vegas (Cambridge, Mass: MIT Press, 1972).

"We began to realize that few of our firm's buildings were complex and contradictory ... Most of the complexities we relished thinking about we did not use, because we did not get big commissions whose programs and settings justified complex and contradictory form," the authors explain, and go on to say that the budgets of the jobs they did get were too low. They conclude, "in general, the world cannot wait for the architect to build his utopia, and in the main the architect's concern ought not to be with what ought to be but with what is..."

Frustrated in their effort to produce an authentic architecture, anxious before ideas that find no social resonance, the authors turn to the city of gamblers, to

33

the perceptions of the lonely and the desperate, to the notion of complex and contradictory architectural decoration. They perceive Las Vegas as an architecture of "the decorated shed," which they describe as "the appliqué of one order of symbols on another." They argue, "Las Vegas shows the value of symbolism and allusion and proves that people, even architects, have fun with architecture that reminds them of something else."

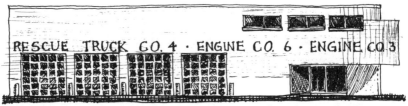

NEW HAVEN, CONN: Dixwell Fire Station (1970).

The design for the Dixwell Fire Station in New Haven, Connecticut is presented in the book along with other examples of the firm's work. The fire station is, in the authors' words, "simple in form -- there are no wings or changes in roof height -- and big in scale -- it contains big elements in a simple bulk." Decoration is limited to a rounded corner and a projecting curve, a change in brick color in a portion of the wall of the apparatus room, a bit of marble at the entrance. There is no appliqué of one order of symbols on another. The building works well and looks like what it is and is not reminiscent of something else.

The authors of Learning from Las Vegas protest against the specialization inherent in industrialized architecture. They argue, "allusion and comment, on the past or present or our own great commonplaces or old clichés, and the inclusion of the everyday in the environment, sacred and profane-- these are what are lacking in modern architecture." But then they turn around and

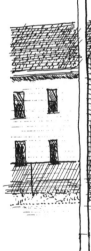

cast admiring glances at the industrialized landscape of the Las Vegas Strip -- its neon signs and speeding cars, at the gambler leaping from one-armed bandit to roulette wheel. Then another turn and they produce the disarmingly honest design of the Dixwell Fire Station.

At the time Learning from Las Vegas was published -- that is, in the early 1970's -- a rash of books appeared featuring photographs of old buildings, all of which were anonymously designed and modestly built: barns, rural churches, handmade houses. In the same way as

IRELAND (near Galway): Long straw thatching, dry stone wall.

Learning from Las Vegas, but less explicitly, these books suggested that the designing of buildings should be a culturally passive activity, a piecing together of cultural symbols and artifacts that are immutable and exist entirely independent of professional architects. In a whole range of judgment about the built environment, these books seemed to identify exact causes and effects, simple and to hand, and, furthermore, to do so without distracting the reader with difficult questions and long analytic arguments from contemplating the illustrations. Unfortunately, a picture

36

of light filtering through the decaying wood wall of an old building, no matter how haunting the image may appear, tells the reader little about the structure of the building, less about its setting, and nothing about the community that built it.

With the increase in the amount of information about the built environment that science and industrial technology have made available to architects, together with new and more complex problems to solve and building techniques to work with, architects might be said to know less and less about more and more and to be increasingly unsure of where architecture either is or ought to be headed.

At the same time the IAUS Idea as Model exhibition catalogue was being prepared for publication, a survey of the work of 23 architects appeared under the title, Post Modern Classicism. The introduction explained:

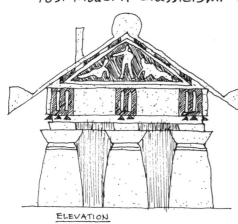

ELEVATION

PLAN VIEW

After a drawing by Robert Venturi (1978).

In the past year [1980] there has been a convergence of styles within Post-Modernism, a convergence towards a manner which could be called classical... Unsympathetic critics would write it all off as "fashion," the recurrence of a conventional style in a time of retrenchment. I don't believe this to be

the case, although fashion is certainly involved. Rather I think it is <u>one</u> logical result of the impasse in which Modernism... has left us... Clearly there are other conventions besides classicism -- Art Nouveau and Vernacular to name two... But the largest movement is Post-Modern Classicism... perhaps a consumer society will not short-circuit this movement and add its corpse to the long list of "isms" it has prematurely turned into "wasms".
(Charles Jencks)

    Four of the architects whose work was viewed from this "classicist" perspective were also represented in the "modernist" IAUS exhibit and all of them had originally gained notoriety through other media-created "isms" that, as the passage quoted above sadly acknowledges, all too quickly turned into "wasms". With a slight twist of stylistic procedure, a "modernist" such as James Stirling or Arata Isozaki or an enamoured observer of the vernacular

HOUSTON, TEXAS: Addition to School of Architecture, Rice University designed by James Stirling (1980). "Modernist" on left, "classicist" on right.

architecture of Las Vegas (Robert Venturi) became a "post-modern classicist".

Modern (as opposed to post-modern) architecture achieved its power as a historical force by penetrating the stylistic appearances of a building in order to confront the structure of the underlying architectural concept:

Absence of verbosity, good arrangement, a single idea, daring and unity in construction, the use of elementary shapes. A sane morality. Let us retain, from these Romans, their bricks and their Roman cement and their Travertine and we will sell the Roman marble to the millionaires... (from "The Lesson of Rome" in Le Corbusier's Towards a New Architecture).

Architecture turned in on itself and in so doing tended to produce bland exteriors of "steel or concrete skeletons, ribbon windows, slabs

BARCELLONA: German Pavilion designed by Mies van der Rohe (1929).

cantilevered or wings hovering on stilts... the raw stuff, so to speak" (from Gropius' introduction to Scope of Total Architecture). The intention was to produce an architecture free of stylistic additives.

39

MODERN

All too often, our real intensions have been and still are misunderstood, namely, to see in the movement an attempt at creating a "style" and to identify every building and object in which ornament and period style seem to be discarded as examples of an imaginary "Bauhaus Style." <u>The object of the Bauhaus was not to propagate any "style," system or dogma, but simply to exert a revitalizing influence on design.</u> A "Bauhaus Style" would have been a confession of failure (from "My Conception of the Bauhaus Idea," emphasis by gropius).

The post-modernist considers the "raw stuff" of architecture, as gropius called it, inarticulate and, therefore, devoid of meaning. Strict procedures of self-development as practiced at the Bauhaus are denounced in Post-Modern Classicism as "elitist and obscure." Such a reaction is inspired by the dream of an architecture that is socially comprehended. This is not to say, however, that the post-modernist is interested in the particulars of the social situation, especially when they are

TACUBAYA, MEXICO: Luis Barragán Residence (1947) interior view.

40

distasteful. The authors of Learning from Las Vegas are careful to explain that they are interested in analyzing Las Vegas "only as a phenomenon of architectural communication" and go on to say that "just as an analysis of a gothic cathedral need not include a debate on the morality

of medieval religion, so Las Vegas' values are not questioned here."

Conscious of the deceptive aspects of such a notion as "post-modern classicism," most of the architects who have drifted into its orbit shy away from anything that might resemble an out-and-out classical revival. The post-modernist is attracted to that area of design in which meaning is so stylized that it cannot be experienced as the specific meaning of a particular architectural style. This is brought about by the eradication of intention.

For example, whether describing one of his "classicist" or "modernist" designs Charles Moore sounds equally ingenuous:

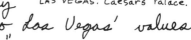

As it was the Piazza d'Italia [New Orleans], paid for by the Italians, we decided to make a fountain in the shape

LAS VEGAS: Caesar's Palace.

NEW ORLEANS: Piazza d'Italia (1979) arch on Lafayette Street.

41

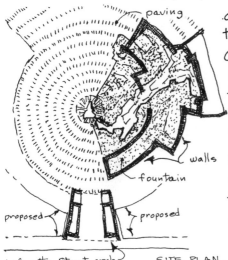

paving

walls

fountain

proposed

proposed

Lafayette Street arch

SITE PLAN

of Italy... I remembered that the architectural Orders were Italian, with a little help from the Greeks, and so we thought we could put Tuscan, Doric, Ionic, and Corinthian columns over the fountain, but they overshadowed it, obliterating the shape of Italy. So instead we added a "Delicatessen Order"... There was a little bit of money left over so we thought we would bang up a temple out front... (from Post-Modern Classicism).

In the Idea as Model exhibition catague he describes his design for a similar urban open space as follows:

The pavilion shown in the model was part of one of the courtyards [in a design for Los Angles' Bunker Hill]. It is simple in form with a semi-circular top, and houses a restaurant. The house form is a reproduction of one of the wonderful Victorians that used to exist on Bunker Hill, half in negative and half in positive. The material is reflective glass.

Using either classical elements, as in the first example, or vernacular elements, as in the second, Moore juxtaposes pieces of the architectural past in such a way as to neutralize their original meaning and reduce them to the status of cultural artifacts.

42

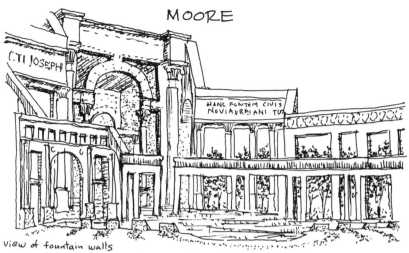

view of fountain walls

Although Moore tends to appear less witty as a "modernist" than he does as a "classicist," both as a writer and designer, the unmistakable undercurrent of a joke is present in both examples. From mocking imitation of the Orders ("the Tuscan Order has water coming down, unfortunately unfluted, but that was the best we could do") down to geographical references ("it would be really swell to place Tiki Torches at the place on the map where Vesuvius would be, but there wasn't enough water to do that"), the details of the two designs and his written description of them resemble bits of a routine delivered by a performer conscious of being on-camera and playing to the crowd.

The joking undercurrent has its origins in the commercial

Delicatessen Order

43

strip that, with the approval of the authors of Learning from Las Vegas, sets up architecture for sale as a commodity. The undercurrent occasionally veers toward more neutral ground where neon-lit parking lots are seen in a less flattering light ("Someday there will be shops around [the Piazza d'Italia], but for the moment it is sitting by itself, and a little lonesome") and where thoughts about architecture as an art are still possible ("from below, [certain details] remind me of some unexecuted Schinkle buildings

After a design proposal for Neue Wache, Berlin (1816) by K.F. von Schinkel.

that I'd seen"). The pain of consciousness, which twists the smile of the post-modernist into a sneer, is revealed for an instant. However, having adapted architecture to the media-generated needs of a consumer society, the designer suppresses the incipient note of protest; the joke retains its primacy.

view of fountain

Like Charles Moore,
Michael Graves is
represented in both the
"modernist" Idea as Model
catalogue and in Post-
Modern Classicism. Unlike
Moore, who performs
this stylistic leap
wearing a fixed grin,
Graves prefers to work
deadpan. He describes
a design for the Sunar
Furniture Showroom as
a procession of partially
remembered details of a
garden promenade:
"pergola, allée, latticed
rooms". The remembered
objects are recorded
as a series of colors
and surfaces such as
those in a painting
and are meant to be
viewed accordingly.
His next composition
is a remembrance,
not of a garden this
time, but of a sixteenth-
century villa suburbana:
"the three stories of
the 'Keystone House' are
reflected in the street
facade, whose
articulation recalls

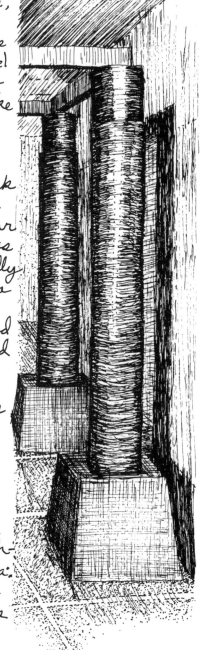

NEW YORK: Sunar Furniture
Showroom (1979) view at entrance.

45

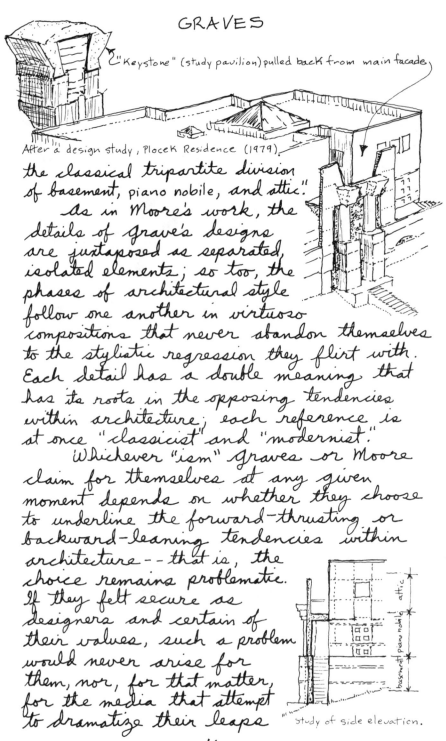

"Keystone" (study pavilion) pulled back from main facade

After a design study, Plocek Residence (1979).

the classical tripartite division
of basement, piano nobile, and attic."

As in Moore's work, the
details of grave's designs
are juxtaposed as separated,
isolated elements; so too, the
phases of architectural style
follow one another in virtuoso
compositions that never abandon themselves
to the stylistic regression they flirt with.
Each detail has a double meaning that
has its roots in the opposing tendencies
within architecture; each reference is
at once "classicist" and "modernist."

Whichever "ism" Graves or Moore
claim for themselves at any given
moment depends on whether they choose
to underline the forward-thrusting or
backward-leaning tendencies within
architecture -- that is, the
choice remains problematic.
If they felt secure as
designers and certain of
their values, such a problem
would never arise for
them, nor, for that matter,
for the media that attempt
to dramatize their leaps

study of side elevation.

from one wobbly "ism" to another. If nothing else, their futile acrobatics demonstrate that there is no general agreement about what direction architecture is taking, what constitutes a valid design, or even what design characteristics are sure to be mediagenic.

Under the circumstances, it is not surprising that Graves chooses to do variations on the Villa Madama -- that is, on a design theme borrowed from an earlier and more secure architecture. The problem is that the procedure works only as a technical exercise.

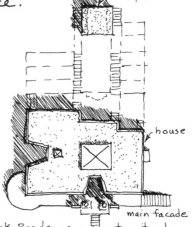

ROME: Villa Madama (c. 1517).

It might be argued that Graves only takes the design of the villa as a starting point, for he reconstructs the theme in different ways in the Plocek residence ("Keystone House") and Kalko residence. However, these designs are nothing more than the original design emptied of its historical significance. As the first great Roman villa of the Renaissance to be built outside the city walls, the Villa Madama had considerable influence and indicated, among

study pavilion

house

main facade

Plocek Residence, schematic site plan.

other things, that Rome had replaced Florence as the cultural capital of Italy. Graves ignores these as well as any more immediate historical factors. He manipulates the formal elements of the design in a kind of shell game that attracts the media's attention away from the hollowness of the bits being maneuvered and toward the maneuver itself. To paraphrase a notion that has traced its own brightly illuminated path from "ism" to "wasm:" the media's attention is the message.

Graves' story and that of the other architects discussed in this essay is the success story of our time. They have courted the media, created mediagenic architecture, and achieved success -- that is, won the approval of the media. All of this is reflected in the way other architects talk about them and their work:

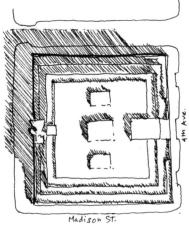

Madison St.

Public Service Building Portland, Oregon (1980), site plan.

I am here to express the feelings of the vast majority of Portland architects about the recommendations of the jury for the Public Service Building competition... The Michael Graves scheme [recommended by the jury] is the cheaper and has the backing of a famous architect [Philip Johnson]... he [Johnson] has become the high "guru" of a coterie of young, gifted people [unnamed but

GRAVES

view from 4th Avenue

including Graves by implication]
who... have discovered that frivolous
means get immediate attention,
and that fashions need not last...
they demolish the hated glass
box and erect the enlarged juke
box or the oversized beribboned
Christmas package, well knowing
that on completion it will be out-
of-date. (Excerpts from an address by Pietro
Belluschi to the City Council on behalf of FAIA,
Portland, Oregon chapter.)

Success -- that is, winning the competition--
means having a design accepted into society,
just as losing the competition means having
it rejected. If Graves achieves success with
a design that to many of his colleagues
resembles an empty Christmas package,
the root of the problem is to be found in
the values of the society that set up the
competition and established its guidelines.
The hollowness of Graves' design for the

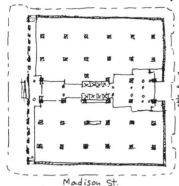

Madison St.
Ground floor plan

Public Service Building,
its assumption of a
stagnant building technology
coated with a veneer of
inflated classical references
-- that is to say, the
emptiness of his success--
is at base economic.
This is what the
authors of Learning from
Las Vegas have to say about the type of
architecture that forms the basis of Belluschi's

49

objection to the architecture produced by graves and the "coterie" he represents:

The structure of Crawford Manor [designed by Paul Rudolph in 1962], which is poured-in-place concrete with concrete block faced with a striated pattern, is a conventional frame supporting laid-up masonry walls. But it does not look it. It looks more advanced technologically and more progressive

NEW HAVEN: Crawford Manor: spatially... We criticize Crawford Manor, not for "dishonesty," but for irrelevance today.

They argue that the type of architecture represented by the work of Rudolph and Belluschi suggests, through its use of modernist imagery, "reformist-progressive social and industrial aims" that it seldom achieves in reality. Seen from this perspective, graves' use of convential structural systems and frivolous appliqué ornament appears to be a more realistic reflection of economic and social conditions. However, as a reflection (cool, detached, uninvolved), it is equally susceptible to the charge of irrelevance.

To understand the great architecture of the past does not mean to recognize the stylistic components of this or that famous facade, but rather the relation between the facade and the underlying structure that produces and justifies it. The challenge for architects today, similar to that which confronted the pioneers of modern architecture, is not to accept and apologize for the lack of relationship between structure and facade but to forge an appropriate structure, redefine the facade, and explore the relationships between them.

SOURCES (in order of appearance in essay)

Kurokawa, Kisho. *Metabolism in Architecture*. London: Studio Vista, 1977.

Benjamin, Walter. *Charles Baudelaire: A Lyric Poet in the Era of High Capitalism*. London: New Left Review Editions, 1968.

Hobsbawm, E.J. *Bandits*. New York: Pantheon Books, 1981.

Boyd, Robin. *New Directions in Japanese Architecture*. New York: Braziller, 1968.

Eisenman Peter, et al. *Five Architects*. London: Oxford University Press, 1975.

Venturi, Robert, Brown, Denise Scott, and Izenour, Steven. *Learning From Las Vegas*. Cambridge, Mass: MIT Press, 1972.

Pommer, Richard. *Idea as Model*. New York: Rizzoli International Publications, 1981.

Jencks, Charles (ed.). *Post-Modern Classicism*. London: Architectural Design and Academy Editions, 1980.

Williams, Raymond. *Television: Technology and Cultural Form*. New York: Schocken Books, 1975.

PART 2 -- MESSAGE FROM THE FIELDS.

Farmstead, 1916.

Farm, mid-1960's.

THE FACTORY IN THE FIELD was a summer-long project, implemented on a small farm owned by and located adjacent to Hampshire College, a small liberal arts college in western Massachusetts, where I was teaching. The farm had been vacant for some time, for it had been purchased and was being reserved for expansion purposes. The objectives of the 'Factory in the 'Field were (1) to develop an approach to architecture that utilizes industrial technology, not to struggle against nature, but to harmonize with its ecological principles; (2) to combine intellectual and manual work in dealing with the group's energy, shelter, and food requirements; (3) to build a sense of community; and (4) to lay the groundwork for establishing the project as a year-round laboratory of ecology, technology, and art.

Three work/study projects focused on (1) the farmhouse, which was redesigned as an academic facility; (2) the barn, which was redesigned as a multi-purpose facility (the first week was devoted to transforming the milking parlor into a design studio); and (3) the land, which

First century, hand-held plow, 5½ hours per acre.

Nineteenth century, riding sulky plow, 4½ hr. per acre.

Twentieth century, tractor and two-furrow plow, 1¼ hour per acre.

Twentieth century, four-axle disk harrow (multi-furrow), ¼ hour per acre.

was replanned to accommodate both industrial and agricultural experiments. While developing proposals for the reuse of the farm, the participants began investigating the traditional building crafts, not from a technical vantage point, but from the point of view of their relation to creative thought.

Work in the design studio and on the farm was supplemented with seminar work that focused on three issues: (1) the function of art in such an undertaking as the Factory in the Field; (2) technology with special attention to energy production and conservation; and (3) the problem and possibilities of small-scale, decentralized industry and agriculture. Time devoted to an organic kitchen garden, workshops on the building crafts, and participation in a visiting artists program rounded out the weekly schedule.

The work day began with a group meeting that reviewed the status of the various projects, determined priorities, and agreed upon a work schedule. Each of the twelve participants had a project, workshop, or seminar for which he or she was responsible; all decisions were made by consensus. The generally cooler mornings were devoted to the three construction projects;

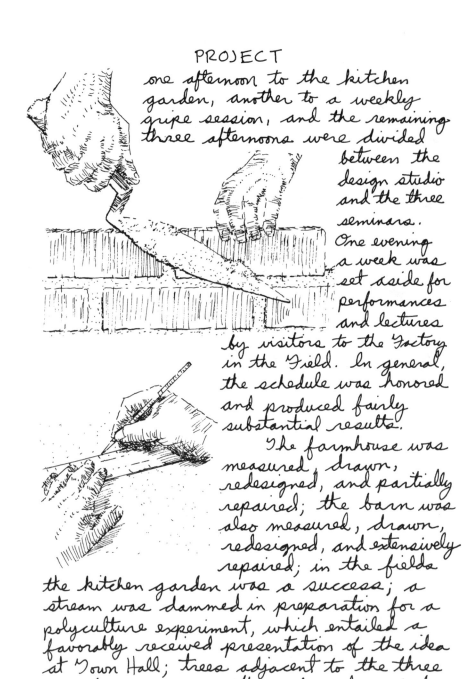

PROJECT

one afternoon to the kitchen garden, another to a weekly gripe session, and the remaining three afternoons were divided between the design studio and the three seminars. One evening a week was set aside for performances and lectures by visitors to the Factory in the Field. In general, the schedule was honored and produced fairly substantial results.

The farmhouse was measured, drawn, redesigned, and partially repaired; the barn was also measured, drawn, redesigned, and extensively repaired; in the fields the kitchen garden was a success; a stream was dammed in preparation for a polyculture experiment, which entailed a favorably received presentation of the idea at Town Hall; trees adjacent to the three project areas were thinned; and previously unmanaged woodlands were explored. The workshops and seminars were organized, reading assigned, questions raised, issues debated. There was a block, however, that resisted our efforts to delve into the problem of the separation of manual from intellectual work.

"I understand that it's the summer, vacation time in the academic calendar," I said at the third or fourth of the weekly gripe sessions. "If you don't want to think, you don't have to. I thought up this program, though I understand there is a feeling among you that this program just happened and simply will go on happening. I disagree."

"We don't need a concept laid on the work we're doing," a student responded and proceeded to voice the opinion held by all but one or two of the participants. "It should be the opposite: the concept should grow out of the work itself and be formulated by those directly engaged in physical labor."

Our efforts were doomed to endless trial and error, for we never formed a clear concept of our relationship as builders to the tools we were using and the structures we

were working on. It was easier and more satisfying to organize and carry out repairs on the barn roof than to rethink the function and design of the structure beneath it. Replacing old shingles was a well-defined task that had immediate results: the roof no longer leaked. Thoughts about alternative uses of the dramatic and slightly mysterious interior were elusive with no clear starting point or conclusion. They seemed to lead nowhere but to other thoughts that, as often as not, circled back on themselves quite unaffected by the changing condition of the roof.

The architectural problem was to find a way, while satisfying the programmatic needs of the Factory in the Field, to sift through the old building relationships and develop a series of new connections, to acknowledge the old structure and, at the same time, make room for new alternatives.

"What would happen if we started with nothing more in mind than the question of what can be done with a pile of bricks?" a member of the group asked in the course of a seminar on the relation between art and technology. A quantity of used bricks had recently been assembled for the repair of the farmhouse foundation. The fact that they were being stored close by may have inspired the question; it certainly inspired the response. It was not long before the group was busily engaged in laying bricks and, in the process, rediscovering traditional brick decorative patterns: the

slot, "X", rectangle, triangle, diamond, "hour glass".

"These bricks and the patterns we're making with them remind me of the shingling we're doing on the barn roof. Can't we do something better than lay down identical rows of identical shingles?" The question of "doing something better" with bricks and shingles led to other questions. What precisely is a brick— that is, of what and how is it made? How is it handled and with what tools? What has been done with brick construction in the past? In light of the development of new building materials and techniques, does the tradionally sized and shaped brick have a valid role to play in anything other than in the preservation of existing brick structures? Why did solely technical answers to such questions seem to be evasive and even, at times, obtrusive? Once again a line of thought was blocked, circled back on itself, and failed to break through the surface of things. "We can use light and dark colored roofing shingles, and lay them in one of the patterns traditionally used in brick-end barns."

    The effort to combine industrial and agricultural work was also frustrated, but for different reasons. By the middle of the summer a number of agricultural activities were being done on a daily basis -- growing food, cutting wood, raising chickens -- and details for expanding these activities were being worked out. Yet, not one activity of an industrial nature, no matter how modest its scope and technical requirements, had been implemented. The

closest the group had come to exploring a subject that related to the factory as opposed to the various field-related issues was to begin asking questions about the tools used in their tree cutting and pruning work. The problem produced a joke: "fine tuning at the Factory in the Field is done with a chain saw and a sledge hammer." The joke, in turn, produced a seminar topic: "one one-thousandth of an inch" and a demonstration of tool grinding, metal shaping, and linear measurement in the college machine shop. The fact remained, however, that the group did not have access to industrial machinery or to the people who know how to use it. This meant that the central

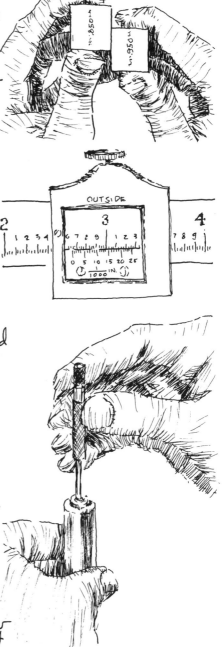

Metalwork measurement: gage blocks (top), vernier scale (middle), small-hole gage (bottom).

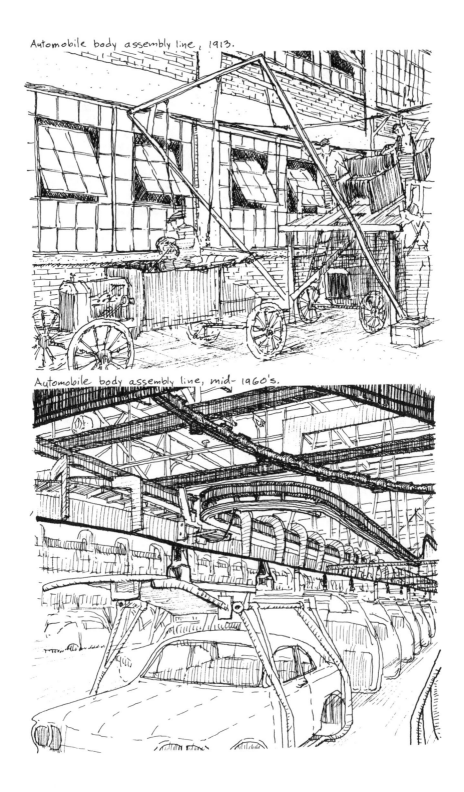

Automobile body assembly line, 1913.

Automobile body assembly line, mid-1960's.

question of the technology seminar could not be dealt with in a satisfactory manner: how to study work and, in particular, the implications of automated work for architecture?

"The Greeks knew about art and sport, but not about work," a seminar participant explained, and pointed out that it was not until the development of the factory system in the nineteenth century that work was conceived as a historical phenomenon to be analyzed in a scientific manner. After

Wrestlers, c. 480 B.C.   Railway workers, c. 1837.

investigating the literature on the subject in the college library, which included recent books and articles on "worker control," the seminar concluded that most of it was concerned with work as seen by managers, not workers. Perhaps the seminar's most rewarding insights grew out of efforts to trace a line from the work done at the Bauhaus in the 1920's back to the Arts and Crafts Movement of the late nineteenth century, especially the work of William Morris. As one participant suddenly realized, "the Factory in the Field is part of an ongoing struggle," and quoting Morris explained:

63

WORK

Until the contrast is less disgraceful
between the fields where beasts live
and the streets where men live, I
suppose that the practice of the arts
must be mainly kept in the hands of
a few highly cultivated men...
(from "The Lesser Arts").

Believing that all the arts "might be
summed up in that one word architecture"
and inspired by John Ruskin's writing,
especially "The Nature of Gothic" in The Stones
of Venice, Morris studied the building crafts
of the Middle Ages and drew up three
"precepts" that became the foundation upon
which the Arts and Crafts Movement and
subsequently the Bauhaus were built:

First, "Art is Man's expression of his joy in
labour." Second, "Nothing should be made
by man's labour which is not worth
making, or which must be made by
labour degrading to the makers." Third,
that the only healthy art is "an art which
is to be made by the people and for the
people, as a happiness to the maker and
the user..." (as summarized by. E.P.
Thompson in his book on Morris).

Arts and Crafts mottoes   c. 1896.

64

WORK

"Ruskin and Morris were the first to set their faces against the tide," Walter Gropius wrote in 1937, but they and "the Arts and Crafts schools for applied art [that] arose mainly in Germany... could not stem the waters... The manufactories still continued to turn out masses of ill-shaped goods while the artist struggled in vain to supply platonic designs. The trouble was that neither of them succeeded in penetrating far enough into the realm of the other to accomplish an effective fusion of both their endeavors." Gropius restated Morris' precepts in his own terms, arguing as follows:

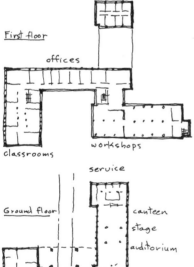

DESSAU: Bauhaus (1925-6), plans.

First floor

studios

offices

classrooms

workshops

Ground floor

service

canteen

stage

auditorium

classrooms

workshops

The only remedy is a completely changed attitude toward work... This attitude no longer perceives the machine as merely an economic means for dispensing with as many manual workers as possible and of depriving them of their livelihood, nor yet as a means of imitating handwork; but, rather, as an instrument which is to relieve man of the most oppressive physical labor and serve to strengthen his hand so as to enable him to give form to his creative impulse... (from "My Conception of the Bauhaus Idea").

Gropius thought highly of the work done at the Bauhaus, but he realized that it could not, by itself, stem the waters any more effectively than the work done by Morris or at the Arts and Crafts schools. "Ideas of cultural import," he said, "cannot spread and develop faster than the new society which they seek to serve."

In response to a growing interest in the Factory in the Field at the college and in the neighboring towns, the participants decided to stage a public progress report mid-way through the summer at which they presented their projects and plans. A message was chalked on a blackboard that was placed at the entrance to the barn, which read:

We have a few dreams. They are in the fields and buildings around you. They are for any one who wants them. Should the number of dreams be insufficient, bring your own dream. The reason for bringing it here is co-operation; without co-operation we cannot keep going.

The barn walls were lined with architectural drawings. A slide show, which was set up to run continuously, illustrated

the progression of the
repair work that had
been done to date.
After explaining a
full-sized mock-up
of construction details
for a new kind of
greenhouse, the
coordinator of the
project conducted a
tour of the field that
was being prepared
for the experiment.
Under the roof of an
outbuilding decorated
with banners designed and made for the
occasion, vegetables from the kitchen garden,
beer, and homemade pretzels were available.
In the farmhouse, photographs indicated the
range of the group's activities: a seminar,
birthday party, lecture-demonstration,
dance performance, poetry reading,
woodworking, dam building, sketching,
singing, barn cleaning.

One of the photographs on display,
taken in the course of a field trip, was
a street scene: one side of the street
was flanked by the brick wall of an
abandoned factory. Faded signs near
a modest doorway in the foreground of
the picture indicated that it had been the
entrance to the shop; an arched entry
in the background had probably led to
offices. There was nothing on the other side

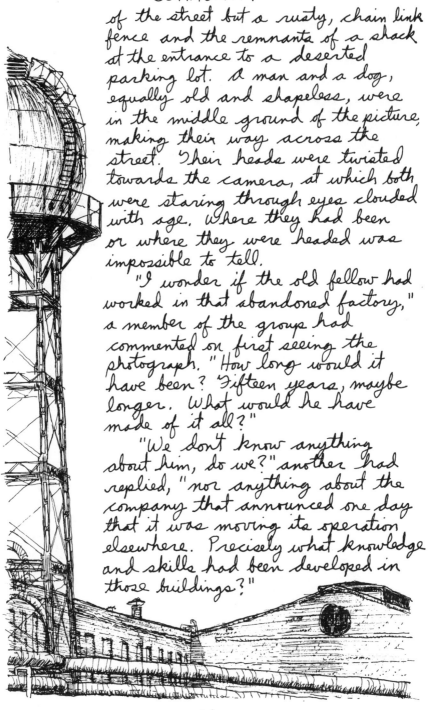

of the street but a rusty, chain link fence and the remnants of a shack at the entrance to a deserted parking lot. A man and a dog, equally old and shapeless, were in the middle ground of the picture, making their way across the street. Their heads were twisted towards the camera, at which both were staring through eyes clouded with age. Where they had been or where they were headed was impossible to tell.

"I wonder if the old fellow had worked in that abandoned factory," a member of the group had commented on first seeing the photograph. "How long would it have been? Fifteen years, maybe longer. What would he have made of it all?"

"We don't know anything about him, do we?" another had replied, "nor anything about the company that announced one day that it was moving its operation elsewhere. Precisely what knowledge and skills had been developed in those buildings?"

COMMUNITY

Joining the discussion, I mentioned that like them, architects had little contact with workers either in the traditional building crafts or newer industrial unions. If there was any meeting at all, it was most likely in the context of a dispute over the introduction of some new (and therefore architecturally intriguing) building material or technique that changed and possibly eliminated existing jobs. Nevertheless, the transition

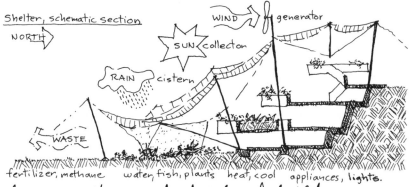

Shelter, schematic section

NORTH

WIND generator

SUN collector

RAIN cistern

WASTE

fertilizer, methane   water, fish, plants   heat, cool   appliances, lights.

from craft to industrialized building construction that Morris feared and Gropius knew was inevitable involved more than a change from hand-operated tools to the power-operated tools of a modern factory. It involved a transformation of the relationship between the elements of the building process that architects, who are specialized construction workers, and their fellow workers must understand equally well.

"This kind of mutual understanding goes far beyond technical considerations," I said, "and presupposes a collective effort that no existing institutional framework either permits or encourages." I then related the following anecdote from my own experiences as a practicing architect:

Conversation with a carpenter. I was leaning against a tree, facing the side elevation of the nearly completed house. Where the drawings indicated a row of projecting mullions for the living room windows of the same rough surfaced hemlock used for the exterior siding, the foreman of the construction crew proposed installing flat pieces of oak.

He had explained that the change would permit the windows to be installed better, which meant in a manner more familiar to him, and that it would not mean changing the windows themselves or their placement. He recalled that the owner had suggested changing the interior trim from smooth hemlock to oak because oak looked better—that is, more expensive. "There's another thing," he had concluded, "those mullions you show on the drawings would stick way out and cut off the view."

I told him that I would think about his proposal.

I walked over to the house,

paused at the front door, and looked at the detailing. It was different from that indicated on the drawings. The foreman had handled the rough exterior and smooth interior hemlock wall surfaces with such attention and skill that the pieces of trim normally used to cover the joint between door jamb and wall could be eliminated.

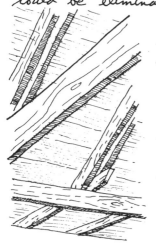

I went down the stairs to the living room and looked up at the ceiling. Again, the detailing was different from that shown on the drawings. The foreman had felt that the joists, which had been sized by engineering tables, "weren't right." Seeing the first few installed, I had agreed and had the joists doubled across the wider span in the middle of the space.

I stepped onto the screened porch, and went out to the diamond shaped column at the outermost point of the house. The foreman had milled the column himself from timber he had searched out at the contractor's mill.

I went inside and called him over to the wall opening in question. "I don't

like the oak strip that you want to put between the windows", I said. "It doesn't relate to the hemlock siding, and it's too thin. It will warp. You installed doors without using any trim. Can you do the same here?"

"Maybe. If I can cut the hemlock right."

I still liked the idea of the original detail, but in the light of the changes that had occurred in the course of construction, the revision seemed appropriate. The foreman and I talked about how the edges of the siding would be finished and decided to cut back the projecting sill.

I explained when I would be coming to the site again and headed for my car. I looked back at the house still dissatisfied. Would the design have been better with collaboration between architect and carpenter from the very beginning?

At the "Factory in the Field" the relationship between the individual and the group, personal and collective work was explored in the seminars on both technology and art; the photograph of the old worker outside the abandoned factory triggered discussions in both of them.

"If one factory worker isn't working, the factory can still operate, but if none of them are working, the place is dead. That's the strength of collective bargaining from the point of view of either the workers or owners of the factory," a participant observed in the course of a seminar, and after a brief pause added, "an artist operates as an individual, not as part of a group, or rather, not part of a group that can affect the commercial aspect of art in such a basic manner." After another and much longer pause, the speaker continued, "yet, all art is social." Referring to material that had recently been discussed in the seminar, she pointed out that the development of architecture in Greece coincided with the beginning of geometry, the building of the gothic cathedrals with the guild system.

"There is no more collective life of the kind that built the monuments of antiquity and the Middle Ages," another participant responded. He suggested that our large buildings

73

and building complexes are built by collections of people whose relationships with one another are quite different in the size and number of operations being accommodated, in the making and erecting of the buildings' components, and in the process of determining which components are appropriate to which operations.

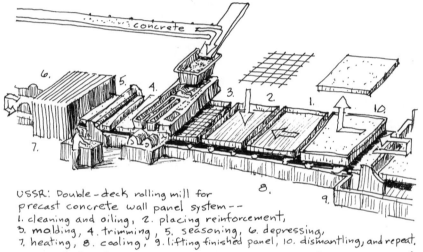

USSR: Double-deck rolling mill for
precast concrete wall panel system --
1. cleaning and oiling, 2. placing reinforcement,
3. molding, 4. trimming, 5. seasoning, 6. depressing,
7. heating, 8. cooling, 9. lifting finished panel, 10. dismantling, and repeat.

"It's the same everywhere in the industrialized world," the speaker said. "Building in the USSR is building in the USA writ large." Drawing on information gathered for the seminar, he explained that industrialization of the construction process was initiated in the Soviet Union in the first half of the 1950's; by the early 1970's three forms of factory production were in operation on a nation-wide basis and two more were being developed. At the time the program was begun approximately fifty million square meters of usable floor space

could be built in a year;
twenty years later that
figure had been doubled.
The building block in
this massive undertaking
was not the traditional
dwelling unit or block of
dwelling units. It was a
micro-district, which
consisted of a mixture of
medical, educational,
recreational, administrative,
and residential facilities
within easy reach of an
industrial district.

Leningrad, Nevsky District.

Tallinn, Mustamaë District.

"You can see small
versions of it detailed for
wood construction in the United States," and
looking towards a nearby window he
muttered, "a curving road, a careful mix
of housing types, a couple of tennis
courts, some picnic tables, a shopping
facility dotted with planters and
advertising 'kiosks,' perhaps a bubbling
fountain." Indicating the photograph of the
old worker and raising his voice, he said,
"that guy isn't there. A suburban subdivision
is inhabited by statistics, by households
with two-point-something children." Lowering
his gaze he concluded angrily, "Bureaucratic!
USSR--USA-- relationships in industrialized
society are strictly controlled."

The issue had been raised before,
usually in the course of a discussion about

community. I pointed out that every type of society has created its own set of organizational problems and groups of specialized workers to deal with them. I related a positive incident about an administrator in the Middle Ages that I had recently read about in a book about gothic architecture (Otto von Simson's The Gothic Cathedral).

In 1194 a fire destroyed a large part of the town of Chartres and all but the west facade of the cathedral. Cardinal Melior of Pisa, papal legate in France, happened to be in the city at the time. According to a chronical written around 1210, he was to a considerable extent responsible for changing the mood of the townspeople and cathedral chapter from despair to renewed faith.

After a drawing in the Musée de Chartres.

The cardinal had helped facilitate a recent organizational reform that placed administration of the chapter's revenues directly under its own authority. He now encouraged the bishop and chapter to commit a sizable sum to the rebuilding program. In urging reconstruction of the cathedral, the cardinal pointed out that the continued prestige and prosperity of both the town and cathedral was dependent on the cult of the Virgin and therefore on the speedy rebuilding of "her special residence on earth."

He then chose an appropriate feast day and called an assembly of the townspeople. His tearful plea for reconstruction was followed by a solemn procession of the bishop and chapter, carrying the sacred

Tunic of the Virgin, which
up to this moment was generally
believed to have been destroyed
in the fire. The cardinal's
message was clear: the Virgin
herself must have permitted
the destruction of the old
basilica because she wanted
a new and more beautiful
church built in her honor.
Inspired by this vision,
the builders of the cathedral
erected a new structure
in about 25 years -- a
miraculously short time;
a miraculous building,
perhaps the most inspiring
of the great gothic cathedrals.

At the Factory in the
Field the notion of community
past, present, and future
was investigated not only
in the seminars but also
in the design studio. The
drafting tables were
littered with abandoned
sketches which had
originated with the fancy
that community was
something that might be

DESIGN

designed. Occasionally one of these sketches was picked up again and something made of it wholly different and possibly more realizable than the original idea.

Image: a planted field, a road, a bridge, a town. Main Street. A five-story building constructed at the end of the nineteenth century. The masonry facade is rusticated on the ground floor. On the upper stories the masonry is carved into rectangular panels beneath the windows, arched panels above the topmost windows, and a classical cornice. In front of the old facade a new skin -- a mixture of transparent, translucent, and reflective glass panels.

A building within a building. Broken images seen in the scattered panels of reflective glass: the play of sun and shade on the fields across the river, cars and trucks crossing the bridge, an adjacent building under construction. Translucent glass panels glow softly at night. Insulated metal louvers, located behind the panels of clear glass, angled to receive the winter sun, then closed at night.

DESIGN

During the summer, the louvers angled to shade the masonry, the air space vented.

The past visible behind the present. Nineteenth-century construction seen through twentieth-century technology. A juxtaposition of surfaces and shapes, of the tangible materials of past and present out of which the future is constructed. Architecture of movement and change.

The object of the 'Factory in the Field was to change the way things get built -- that is, to change the relationship between the processes of design and construction. This effort focused on a specific set of relationships in the built environment: factory and farm. In other words, an effort was made to make the notion of creativity specific and to extend it to the basic work processes. Soon after the inception of the 'Factory in the Field it became evident that in any talk about creating architecture, about being architecturally creative, a number of different things were being referred to.

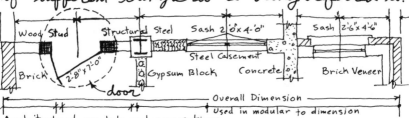

Architectural symbols and conventions.

DESIGN

At the simplest level, the notion of creating a design was clearly a kind of recreation. Through the use of specific notations and drawing conventions a building of a particular type was reproduced --

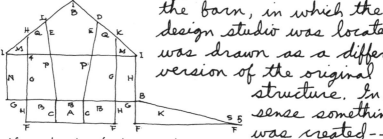

After a drawing of a barn made in 1838.

the barn, in which the design studio was located, was drawn as a different version of the original structure. In a sense something was created -- not a barn, as such, but a notated barn. The designer may have attempted to record the actual barn as completely and accurately as possible; however, this process was necessarily a simplification, by sheer fact of scale reduction if nothing else. Only certain features of the structure were recorded, and these were transcribed into a series of drawing conventions -- a door, for example, transcribed on a

floor plan into a single line, its swing into an arc. These selected elements were then projected into imagined situations -- the wall in which the door was located was redrawn in some way or erased altogether. This process was creative, but not beyond the basic level of producing a set of architectural drawings.

The next level of architectural creativity occurred when in the midst of scraping off accumulated layers of dirt and attempting to repair one of the barn walls, the designer began to view it from a different vantage point. The wall that had been drawn, erased, altered, and redrawn suddenly seemed to come into focus. Its features, which until now had simply been recorded, suddenly seemed to stand out in sharp relief. It was no longer just a wall, but a particular wall. The boards of which it was made were of different lengths and widths, and their edges were not parallel. The vertical supports to which the boards were attached were also irregular. At the same time, large

sections of the wall were hinged panels
that despite irregularities of construction
and years of neglect still functioned.
These characteristics precluded the use
of drafting equipment and techniques
that depend on regularity and expanded
the design options. In other words, the
process of simultaneously recording
and repairing the wall began to make
unexpected demands, which led to a
heightening of creative attention.

    For one designer the wall became
another kind of fence in the farm complex.
He examined other fences in other contexts
built of other materials. He read about
fences, drew and photographed fences,
thought about fences and the relation
between the spaces they bounded. He then

developed a series of free standing, self-
supporting walls in various contexts:
agricultural, industrial, institutional,
residential. Having been inspired in part
by the work of French architect and
industrial designer Jean Prouvé, he called
the series an "alphabet of walls." This
alphabet was adopted by a design group
and formed the basis of a series of site
studies indicating the incremental development
of the Factory in the Field.

   Another designer focused on the gaps
between the irregular boards of the same
wall. For her the wall resembled a veil.
She studied lattices and screens, especially
in the context of the architecture of the
Middle East, and constructed a series of

FEZ: Sahrij Madrasa, entrance screen detail.

84

grilles in different
materials. Her idea
of wall veil was
developed further in
a series of design
proposals for converting
the barn into a
multi-purpose facility,
the veils being
designed to suggest
the nature of the
various activities and
their interrelationship.
    Both the alphabet
of walls and the
concept of wall veils
were developed into
projects that involved
changes in the
daily schedule of
the Factory in
the Field.
Each of these
design ideas
was significant,
for each of them
deepened understanding
of a specific
architectural element
and what it would
mean to change it.
    The Factory in
the Field was a
short-lived,

isolated struggle unknown except to the small number of people whose lives it touched. It indicated a different approach to architecture from that required by professional practice. During my final tour of the projects, the coordinator of the work at the barn felt it appropriate to explain, "When I was younger I wrote poetry. At some point I became shy about sharing it with others. Not long after that I stopped writing altogether. Well, in the course of the summer I started writing again. I wanted you to know."

I was pleased but perplexed. I could sense but not explain the connection between this kind of creative practice and the collective activity that had given rise to it. I neither asked nor was told the subject matter of the writing. I doubted that it related to the specific task of repairing the barn, but at the same time, I was sure it had somehow evolved out of everyday communication about such problems as insect-infested wood and defective masonry work. Perhaps words had changed for the barn worker/poet, taking on social and material as well as personal and abstract meaning. What came to mind was an image of the continuum of human creativity ranging from the lonely struggle to imagine a building to the communal effort to bring it to life.

SOURCES

Gropius, Walter. *Scope of Total Architecture.*
New York: Collier Books, 1962.

Lukács, Georg. *History and Class Consciousness.*
Cambridge, Mass.: MIT Press, 1971.

Marx, Karl. *Capital.* Moscow: Progress
Publishers, 1963.

Thompson, E.P. *William Morris: Romantic
to Revolutionary.* New York: Pantheon
Books, 1976.

von Simson, Otto. *The Gothic Cathedral.*
New York: Harper Torchbooks, 1964.

Weil, Simone. *The Need For Roots.* New York:
Harper Torchbooks, 1971.

Williams, Raymond. *The Country and the City.*
New York: Oxford University Press, 1973.

Zhukov, K., Fyodorov, V. *Housing Construction
in the Soviet Union.* Moscow: Progress
Publishers, 1974.

PREFACE. As the sterile historicism that permeates the pages of our architectural journals demonstrates on the one hand, and the bleak building masses that increasingly dominate the skyline of our cities demonstrate on the other, every architectural message from the past that is not truly recognized by the present is threatened with being hopelessly blurred or erased altogether.

The following essay was inspired by a passage in John Summerson's book, The Classical Language of Architecture, in which the circular temple is presented as an architectural theme that has been developed in different ways in different eras. I extended the historical sequence presented by Summerson both backward and forward in time and adapted it to an investigation of the relationship of building design to building construction across the ages. I was concerned with two interrelated questions about the architecture of the past: (1) how symbolic thought and the development of architecture as a language did or did not relate to practical thought and the development of building technology; (2) the presence or absence of a relationship between the people who designed the sequence of buildings and the ideas they had in mind and the people who built those buildings and the tools they had at hand.

ENGLAND. STONEHENGE. Physical struggle and spiritual transcendence exist side by side in the organization of frightful boulders. The towering masses glisten darkly, more like metal than stone. Their sombre gleam suggests a tall city built of iron.

A circle 350 feet in diameter was dug into a desolate chalk plain. Then a ditched and banked avenue was added, connecting the circle with the adjacent river, and the great stones erected. Thirty-odd upright stones, averaging 26 tons each, carried a ring of gigantic stone lintels in a circle within the earthen circle. In the center was a flat stone altar;

around the altar, upended stones in various configurations. Most of these inner stones, some weighing as much as 40 tons, were apparently transported 150 miles -- no one knows how. Two rings of pits outside the outer ring suggest the scheme was never fully realized, that even more boulders were to be erected.

The tenaciousness of the builders of Stonehenge can be felt in hard surfaces grooved by the pounding strokes of heavy stone hammers. Their respect for work can be seen in the representation of their tools carved in one of the central uprights. Their tie to the past is revealed in details which must have been adapted from earlier wooden structures. For example, the lintels are secured to each other with a tongue-and-groove joint and to the uprights with a mortice-and-tenon connection at each end. Their reach toward the future is suggested in the profile of the upright stones, which taper toward the top with a slight convex curve, foreshadowing the profile of the classical column.

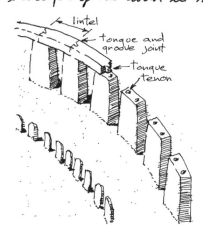

Thought
and physical
work exist
side by side--
here in
contradiction,
there in
harmony --
producing an
architectural
statement in
which life
hangs in
the balance.

THE ROMAN EMPIRE. The face of the
quarry slanted upward 80 feet or more --
dull, broad, flat -- scored with horizontal
rows of delicate and regular chisel
marks. The work was done by slaves
and prisoners of war, as many as 7,000
at a time, under a blazing, silent sun
and cloud of dry, abrasive marble dust.
Dull tapping and scraping of mallets
and chisels, panting breaths, moans
and sighs were the only sounds.

A groove was cut around each
large, rectangular block of marble and
wooden wedges inserted which were then
saturated with water. The edges of the blocks
reflecting the hot sun, shimmered as they
were worked loose. The marble was brought

down roughly paved roads in wooden slides, then dragged on sleds, and for short distances rolled in wooden frames.

The blocks were treated with great care and precision. The jobs that were done, the tools that were used could be sensed in the marble surface: hammering (hammers, mallets, and mauls); cutting, splitting, and scraping (wedges, saws, and chisels); boring (bow-drills); grasping and holding (pincers, vises, and brakes); sharpening (grindstones, whetstones, and saw-sharpening tools); measuring and marking (rules, squares, plumb-lines, compasses, and calipers).

ROME: the temple of Vesta (First Century B.C.).

ROME. TEMPLE BY THE TIBER. For the round temple by the Tiber River built in the first century B.C. known as a temple of Vesta, the Roman goddess of the hearth, the blocks of marble were sawn into alternating tall and shallow courses with graded heights, the courses at the base of the wall being taller and less finished than those above. The design of the upper courses described the process whereby the edges of the wall blocks and ends

Temple by the Tiber, partial elevation.

97

of the column flutes were carved before
erection, while the remainder of the finish
work was done in place : the edges of the
blocks were made smooth, the remainder
rough textured.

    The suffering of the
slaves who built the
temple was turned into
an elegant dance of
Corinthian columns around
a void, a memory of the
earliest shelter, the cave, the circular hut
with its central fire.

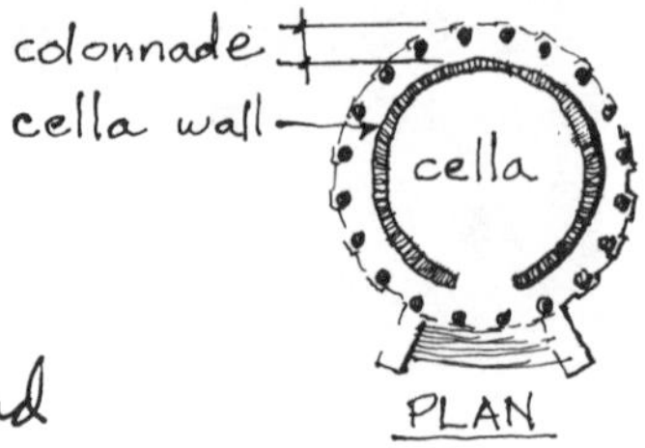

colonnade

cella wall

cella

PLAN

BUILDING IN THE MIDDLE AGES. The manorial system of the middle ages with its small domains which met their own agricultural needs, did their own simple manufacturing on the spot, and engaged in little trade reduced the severity of the class divisions of the Roman Empire. It produced a set of conditions in which manual labor reached new heights of

After a design in stained glass, Chartres Cathedral (1194-1220).

After details in Bruegel's painting, THE LARGE TOWER OF BABEL.

accomplishment and social regard. The gradual development of trade and of trade centers produced a guild system which was the first strong organization of craft workers, and a set of conditions in which artisans, for the first time in world history, became respected members of society. Certain social relations of the past began to fade along with some of the mystical prejudices and superstitions.

Craft workers with rights and privileges guaranteed by the guilds had both the opportunity and incentive to investigate, experiment, improve the old tools, invent new ones, and develop new technical methods. Their ability to migrate contributed to the diffusion of discoveries and the pooling of experience.

Craft lore bore the seeds of the first international sciences but remained craft lore. The practical science of craft workers such as smiths and miners was still largely undifferentiated from the impractical tradition of magic, in which it was imbedded. Furthermore, the transmission of such lore was through the system of apprenticeship -- that is, it was largely imitative and therefore conservative. Finally, craft lore was liable to be secret, for the guilds jealously guarded the mysteries of their crafts.

Chartres Cathedral, south rose window.

RENAISSANCE. BRAMANTE'S TEMPIETTO.

The clearing in front of the church of Saint Peter in Montorio was filled with a motionless, silent crowd. Occasionally a ripple of movement generated by a group of new-comers trying to force their way towards the cloister at the side of the church would gradually fade into the solid resistance of those who were massed behind the barrier that had been erected in front of the church. Most of the crowd were artisans and shopkeepers. Within the cloister itself Bramante's Tempietto, a memorial to the martyrdom of Saint Peter, built on the site where the event was believed to have taken place, was being unveiled.

ROME: S. Pietro in Montorio, as it was at the end of the fifteenth century.

TEMPIETTO

ROME: the tempietto (1502).

What had been "shelter" in the temple by the Tiber was "post" in Bramante's version of the same architectural theme. Bramante eliminated all sense of space, of shelter, by cutting the width of the enclosed area (cella) nearly in half, doubling its height, and capping it with a hemispherical dome.

He inserted a molded plinth
beneath the colonnade and
substituted the Doric for the
Corinthian order. Based on
the authority of the Roman
architect Vitruvius, Bramante
believed that in the invention
of the Doric order the ancients
had "borrowed manly beauty,
naked and unadorned," while
the Corinthian order was "an
imitation of the slenderness
of a maiden." He inscribed
a series of verticals on
the cella wall and originally
may have intended to extend
the strong verticals of the
colonnade into the upper
story by replacing the
balusters above the columns
with rectangular posts.

    A shock of expectation
suddenly passed through
the crowd. The monotonous
wail of a psalm had
ceased and a low, clear

ATHENS: Erechtheion (c.420B.C.),
Karyatid.

voice could now be heard: "Miseratur vestri..." Some of those closest to the barriers and here and there further off fell to their knees. The great majority, however, remained standing, their heads erect. The voice continued, rising higher and yet clearer; more and more heads bowed. But there were those who resisted the impulse to kneel.

"The building was built with our sweat, not with their drops of water," a voice muttered angrily.

"It's the truth, friend. And answer me, who erected the barrier that now separates us from that which we built?" another voice responded.

Yet, by the time the benediction was being intoned, "Benedicat vos omnipotens Deus," every head had been lowered.

BAROQUE. BERNINI AND BORROMINI.

After Carlo Maderno's death in 1629, Gianlorenzo Bernini took over as architect to St. Peter's. Francesco Borromini had worked there for ten years, first as a draftsman and stonecarver, then as a designer and overseer of various details of the ornamental work. Respecting Borromini's technical knowledge and skills if not his already distinctly personal work as a designer, Bernini made him an assistant.

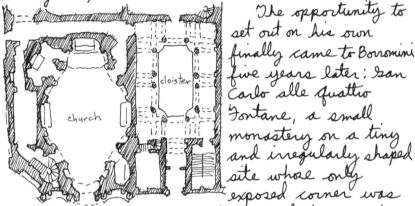

ROME: S. Carlo alle Quattro Fontane (1638-41).

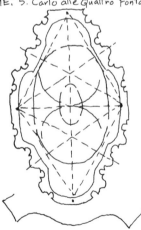

Plan of church showing geometric scheme.

The opportunity to set out on his own finally came to Borromini five years later: San Carlo alle Quattro Fontane, a small monastery on a tiny and irregularly shaped site whose only exposed corner was reserved for one of the four fountains that defined the street intersection. The extraordinary ingenuity and character of Borromini's design for the interior was immediately recognized. His career was launched; his reputation established. For the next thirty years he produced

106

designs that were invariably considered ingenious but odd and at times bizarre. Setting the highest professional goals for himself, but tortured and ever more reclusive, Borromini's career ended in suicide. His last work, begun in 1665 and substantially completed in 1667, the year of his death, was the facade of San Carlo.

Bernini's Sant' Andrea al Quirinale, 1658-70, is located on the same street as San Carlo. The facades of the two churches were designed about the same time; both were inspired by the facade Michelangelo had designed in 1546 for the twin palaces on the nearby Capitoline Hill. Both Bernini and Borromini were intrigued by the way Michelangelo had juxtaposed two classical orders at entirely different scales: a large Corinthian order supporting a noble entablature and between the Corinthian pilasters a small order of Ionic columns supporting a miniature entablature.

Bernini took a single bay of

ROME: Sant' Andrea al Quirinale (1658-70), plan.

large order

small order

ROME: Palazzo dei Conservatori (1546).

107

Michelangelo's design and set the small order spinning first around the oval shape of the church and then out through the large Corinthian pilasters to form a porch at the entrance. Bernini's sinuous line is a simple variation on Michelangelo's theme, easy to follow, pleasant to contemplate.

Borromini's facade for San Carlo consists of three bays. In the lower tier two concave outside bays and a convex center bay are tied together by an

Sant'Andrea al Quirinale, facade.

unbroken, undulating entablature. In the upper tier all three bays are concave, the entablature is broken into three segments, and further broken by the design of the oval medallion. Below, the small columns of the outside bays frame wall panels and support statue niches. Above, the small columns frame niches and support wall panels. This system of reversal

Study of the facade of San Carlo alle Quattro Fontane, after a drawing by Borromini.

SAN CARLO

continues into the central
bays, where the recessed
door and sculpture
niche of the lower tier
is answered above by a
projecting oval volume
and the loosely attached
medallion.

This composition of
broken rhythms is the
culmination of a cycle of
theoretical research
on the curved wall
surface which began
with the design for
the interior of San
Carlo at the very
beginning of Borromini's
career as an independent
architect. It articulates
a combination of
scientific and religious
thought still alive in
the old and despairing
architect -- condemned,

San Carlo alle Quattro Fontane,
facade (1665-67).

at this point in his career, to public indifference
and professional isolation. His use of the
curve is mathematically complex (based on
three aligned triangles) and, at the same
time, philosophically appropriate (Three and
One together). Neither the eye nor the mind is
allowed to rest; neither intuition nor reason
can solve the riddle.

SAN CARLO

The use of architecture as a language has implied, at all times, that it has achieved eloquence, a particular attitude towards history. Bernini and Borromini could not have used Michelangelo's juxtaposed orders of contrasting scales without believing, each in his own way, that the detail embodied an architectural principle that transcended the moment of its invention, that the moment of its invention existed in a past charged with the present. The specific detail, taken out of the Capitoline palaces, out of Michelangelo's life work, was preserved in the facade of both Sant'Andrea al Quirinale and San Carlo alle Quattro Fontane and, at the same time, reinvented.

LONDON. END OF THE SEVENTEENTH CENTURY. CHRISTOPHER WREN AND THE DOME OF ST. PAUL'S CATHEDRAL. Time of the Navigation Acts. England was becoming a sea power. Its economy was being transformed. The vestiges of feudalism were being absorbed and transformed by mercantile capitalism: "trade" was replacing the word "craft."

LONDON: after a seventeenth-century illustration (before the Great Fire).

Old St. Paul's

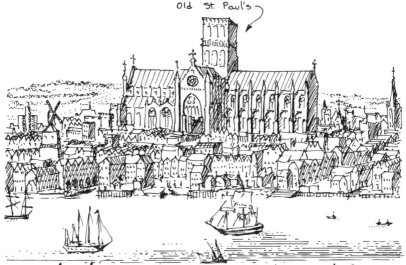

Christopher Wren began work on St. Paul's in 1666 not as an architect but as a highly respected scientist. He was asked to survey the condition of the existing medieval structure and the classical facing which Inigo Jones had designed for it 30 years earlier. Wren had just returned from a trip to Paris where his interest in both practical and theoretical architectural questions led him to seek out and talk with artisans as well as architects, painters, and sculptors, and to study the latest building techniques from

the laying of foundations to the gilding of
ceilings. He had been struck especially by the
domes which crowned many
of the new buildings. In his
report he carefully explained
what was wrong with St.
Paul's and how it could be
corrected, and argued that the
old central tower, the remnant
of a Gothic steeple which
had been destroyed by
fire in the previous century,
should be removed and a
dome erected in its place.
His proposal was accepted
in August, but within a
few weeks the great Fire
of London changed everything.

Design for domed crossing for old St. Paul's, 1666.

    Wren became involved in the rebuilding of
the city. He submitted a renewal plan which
indicated symbolically what the city was to
become in reality: in his plan nearly all the
principal streets converged upon a stock
exchange which was located in the center of a
formal open space surrounded by monumental

Plan for the rebuilding of the city, 1666.

commercial buildings. With equal frankness, the cathedral was shown considerably reduced in size.

For 16 years Wren designed, oversaw the accounts, and supervised construction of 51 of the 87 parish churches which had been destroyed in the Fire. St. Paul's involved him in an even broader range of tasks that took over 40 years to complete. Similarly, the majority of master craft workers that Wren engaged, as well as many of their employees, devoted most of their working lives to the construction of the new cathedral. Their work

St. Bride, Fleet Street, 1670-84; spire, 1702-3.

like his required a willingness to experiment, for none of these people, including Wren, had ever been involved in such a large undertaking. Furthermore, they were working with a new architectural style, a blend of the Classical and the Baroque, which presented new problems of engineering and weather resistance.

Developing the design

St. Paul's, Greek Cross design, c. 1672.

and overseeing the production
of scale models and detailed
drawings of each section of
the work represented only part
of Wren's work. From the
beginning he was involved
with fund-raising. (At one
point he got himself elected
to Parliament to help
ensure the renewal of a
tax earmarked for the
cathedral.) The expenditure
of funds concerned him
no less. (He scrutinized
the accounts each month
and negotiated wages,
prices, contracts, and
loans.) Demolition of
the old structure was
carried out under his
supervision. (For part of
the work he developed a
battering-ram; for another,
a system using explosives.)
He supervised the excavation
(for archeological as
well as constructional
purposes) and organized
the small site to
accommodate the various
crafts (which meant
timing the delivery of
materials as well as
allocating the limited

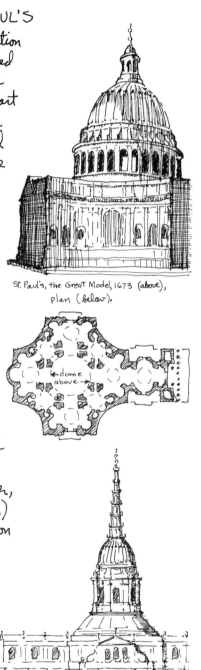

St. Paul's, the Great Model, 1673 (above),
plan (below).

St. Paul's, the Warrant Design, 1675.

114

ST. PAUL'S

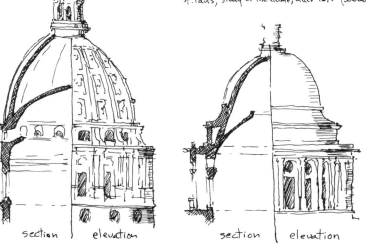

section | elevation   section | elevation

amount of storage space). He even performed the
duties associated with his official title, Surveyor.
   On the basis of thoughtful observation and
regular consultations with the artisans, Wren
adapted the design to their skills and special knowledge.
(For example, he originally wanted a single-tiered
portico at the main entrance, but discovering that the
quarry was probably incapable of producing
blocks of stone large enough, he adopted a

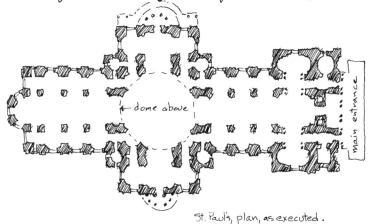

St. Paul's, plan, as executed.

115

two-tiered solution.) At the same time he learned from the artisans. Together they developed new techniques in almost every craft and "standards of workmanship which, once attained, remained the pride of English building for a century" (Summerson).

All the problems relating to load bearing and weight distribution were Wren's responsibility: soils investigation and site drainage; foundations; scaffolding; long-span construction in timber, brick, and stone; the dome. Disputes and difficulties were referred to him. (He once spent 12 days on a trip to the Island of Portland to help rearrange the quarrying operation which had broken down.) Then there were the meetings -- he had to reconcile the needs of the Church with those of the Crown with those of Parliament with those of his art.

stone lantern

outer dome of timber and lead

intermediate dome
(structural cone of brick
to support lantern)

oculus

inner masonry dome

double chain (---)

Cutaway drawing showing the construction of the dome.

116

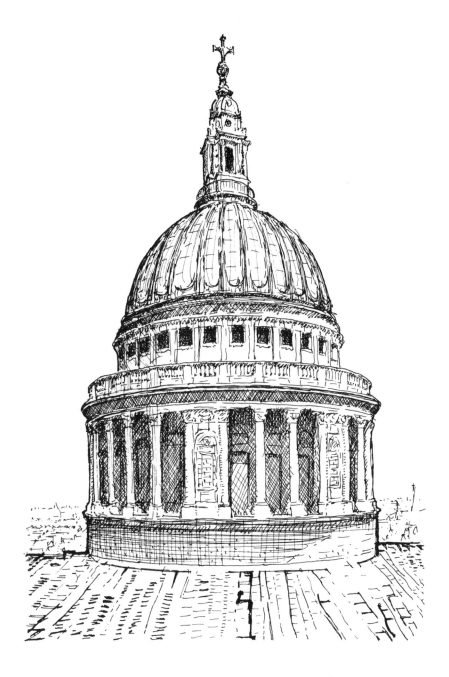

YORKS.: Mausoleum at Castle Howard (1729-42).

EIGHTEENTH CENTURY. THE MAUSOLEUM AT CASTLE HOWARD was designed in 1728 by Nicholas Hawksmoor, Christopher Wren's pupil and then valued assistant. The mausoleum is situated on a lonely rise in the park; its silhouette appears dark and meditative against the sky. Compared to the design of Wren's dome of St. Paul's, Hawksmoor's version of the same architectural theme appears grim. The airiness and buoyancy of St. Paul's dome is gone; the colonnade is close and tense. "Doorway" as an architectural element is separated from its normal meaning and set spinning around the enclosed space: only one of the four frames actually contains a door. The interior wall surface presses

118

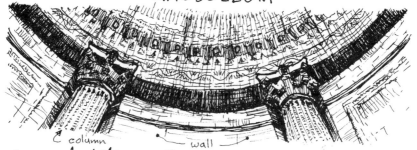

column   wall

inward between the columns. The light
inside is shadowless. At dusk, it begins
to fade. Things outside grow dim and
distant: the main house with its courts
and monumental gateways and the park
with its architectural ornaments. The
mausoleum forces the
attention inward and
downward.

This was the last
structure to be built at
Castle Howard. A
worried Charles Howard,
3rd Earl of Carlisle,
relayed to Hawksmoor
a scholarly criticism
by Lord Burlington, who
was regarded by his
contemporaries as the
foremost authority on
classical architecture:
there was no precedent
in antiquity for the
narrow spacing of the
colonnade columns.
Hawksmoor dictated
and sent off seven

pages of justification, which concluded that antique or not the spacing was right for the purposes of the design and could not be altered "tho' I be hired to do it."

Hawksmoor died in 1736 before the mausoleum was completed. A staircase was added to the upper platform, modeled on one Burlington designed for the addition to his family residence. An auction of nearly two thousand of Hawksmoor's drawings that was held in 1740 drew little attention. Burlington was there, but only to acquire Hawksmoor's collection of drawings done by the seventeenth-century English architect, John Webb. The vast majority of Hawksmoor's own drawings were ignored, then lost.

In Christopher Wren's work the wall was something onto which elements of the classical language of architecture were attached. Hawksmoor was concerned with the wall itself as an expressive element. Towards the end of the eighteenth century,

After a drawing by A.L.T. Vaudoyer (1785). " The idea of spherical houses, like all the other fantastic projects of the revolutionaries, resulted from the restlessness of the period" (Emil Kaufmann).

ideas about architectural form remarkably similar to Hawksmoor's began to appear in designs, not for aristocratic estates, but for buildings in another context: City gate, Hall of the Convention, Public Library, Theater, Hospital, Pump House, Town House, House of a Laborer... Hawksmoor had anticipated the architectural language of the French Revolution.

PARIS: Tollhouse designed by Claude-Nicholas Ledoux (1784-89).

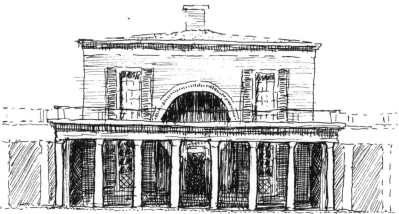

CHARLOTTESVILLE: University of Virginia, Pavilion IX designed by Thomas Jefferson (1821).

NEW HAVEN: In the opening years of the twentieth century the architectural firm of Carrère and Hastings was still detailing hand-carved stone and marble surfaces for Yale University's Memorial Hall. At the same time, however, the firm was working on the first long-span, all-steel suspension bridge of the century, the Manhattan Bridge in New York City.

NEW YORK CITY: Manhattan Bridge (1901-09).

It was the time of the Spanish-American War -- a time of military parades and pageants, statues and monuments. It was the time

that the country's largest manufacturer of crude steel was in the process of combining with the largest companies making finished steel products to form the first billion-dollar corporation, U. S. Steel.

CHICAGO: Dynamo exhibit in Louis Sullivan's Transportation Building (1893).

122

NEW HAVEN: Yale, Memorial Hall (1901-02).

With its inflated dome, tall windows, loosely spaced columns, and busy doorways, this memorial, whose walls are inscribed with the names of battles and Yale graduates who died in the nation's wars, was more a celebration of war than a somber remembrance of its victims. Memorial Hall's rusticated ground floor with one column interval accented by a combination of doorway and window and the other by the detailing of the dome

OXFORD: James Gibbs' Radcliffe Library (1749).

recalled the playful Radcliffe Library at Oxford, designed in the mid-eighteenth century by James Gibbs, a contemporary of Nicholas Hawksmoor. Drawings in the Yale Alumni Magazine at the time Memorial Hall was being built indicate that Carrère and Hastings originally intended to use Radcliffe Library's paired columns as well. The aggressive fragmentation of Gibbs' design may have been preserved, but not its wit. A wry smile became a fixed grimace.

CHICAGO: Columbian Exposition, "White City" (1893).

A sordid military adventure to obtain the holdings of Spain, the most decrepit colonial power in Europe, was draped in the mantle of classicism. The quiet formation of giant corporations such as U.S. Steel was hidden behind the blare of patriotism. The harsh

CHICAGO: industrial city (c. 1890).

reality of the industrial city was veiled by the image of "White City," the name given to the ensemble of classical revival buildings in Chicago's Columbian Exposition of 1893 that encouraged designs such as Yale's Memorial Hall.

When the bar was white-hot he seized it with his tongs and with his hammer Knocked it into regular lengths on the anvil tapping gently as though it were glass. Then he put sections back in the fire, whence he took them out one by one to work them up. He was making hexagonal rivets. He put the pieces into a heading frame, flattened the top to make a head, tapped the six sides, then threw down the finished rivets, still red-hot, and they gradually darkened and faded out on the black floor. He did the operation with unbroken hammering, swinging a five-pound hammer in his right hand, finishing a detail with each tap, turning and working the iron so skillfully that he could go on talking and looking at people. The anvil gave out a silvery ring. Without a drop of sweat and perfectly comfortable, he banged away happily,

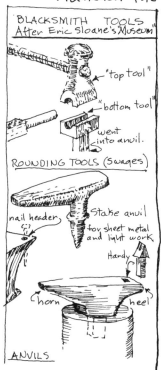

BLACKSMITH TOOLS
After Eric Sloane's "Museum"

"top tool"

"bottom tool"
went into anvil.

ROUNDING TOOLS (swages)

nail header

Stake anvil
for sheet metal and light work

Handy

horn   heel

ANVILS

preen

poll

eye

face

Swage
hammer

HAMMERS

Hammer Tongs

Hoop Tongs

TONGS

into
anvil

BEAK IRONS

Flat Bit

Round Bit

BITS

apparently with no more
effort than when he cut out
his paper pictures in the
evening at home.

"Oh, this is the little
twenty millimeter rivet," he
said in answer to a question.
"You can do up to three
hundred of them a day.
But you have to keep in
practice because your arm
soon gets rusty."

[Later, on a break he
went into a shed] where
the boss was installing
quite an elaborate plant...
He came to a halt in
front of one of the rivet
machines, and there he

126

MEMORIAL

stood dreaming with bowed head and attentive eyes. The machine was turning out 44-millimeter rivets with the unruffled ease of a giant. And indeed nothing could be simpler. The stoker took the piece of iron out of the furnace, the stoker placed it in the frame which was continually watered so as to keep the steel tempered, and the job was done, the screw came down and the bolt fell out with its head round as if it had come out of a mold. In twelve hours this blasted plant could turn out hundreds of pounds of rivets...

from Zola: L'Assommoir

The fate of the worker became the fate of society as a whole, including our concept of history. The development from the individual handicraft of a Gothic cathedral to the cooperative handicraft of St. Paul's and from that to machine industry was accompanied by ever greater specialization and rationalization of the work process. Just as work was progressively mechanized and separated from the variable, flowing nature of the human personality, time was frozen into exactly delimited historical periods, fragmented into isolated acts and objects. Architecture was transformed into derivative and static stylistic forms. It was removed from the real life-process.

CHICAGO: Classical facade (masonry) masking structural frame (steel and wrought-iron), (c. 1890).

An architectural firm such as Carrère and Hastings stood helpless before the ever deepening contradiction between the demand of traditional architecture that a building should appear timeless -- as though it always had been and always would be -- and the demand of industrial technology for change. They were helpless because as architects they were no closer to owning the equipment, supplies, land, and capital utilized in their projects than any other construction worker. They owned only their own labor-power, which they presented to their clients as a "professional service" -- that is, as a commodity. Unlike Christopher Wren, Carrière and Hastings began their work by signing a contract that spelled out what they were to do step by step. It is not that Carrière and Hastings were wrong in their work on the design for Memorial Hall -- history (their own Manhattan Bridge) denied the work itself.

MODERN ARCHITECTURE. FRANK LLOYD WRIGHT'S GUGGENHEIM MUSEUM. A colonnade of structural fin walls spirals around a central void that rises to a circular opening capped with a transparent dome. In creating an androgynous version of the architectural theme of the round temple surrounded by a colonnade, Wright's design assumes prophetic intensity.

NEW YORK CITY: Guggenheim Museum, interior view of dome (1943-59).

From the time of Bramante on, the architecture of the West had presented an ever more stylized expression of passion.

130

GUGGENHEIM

The pioneers of modern architecture stripped away the decorative elements and demanded that passion be genuine. They struggled to present passion directly and without disguise through the articulation of structure and function.

Louis Sullivan: "Form follows function."

Frank Lloyd Wright: "Form and function are one."

PLAN

Any reproach against or glorification of the individualism of modern architecture in its early stages of development obscures the social nature of this individualism. The criticism Wright directed towards conventional architectural

SECTION

decoration and towards social convention were of a piece. Wright is reported to have complained at the conclusion of a tour of a university, "How could anyone get a liberal education in such illiberal buildings?"

In a design such as that for the Guggenheim

GUGGEHEIM

Museum, Wright developed a
new function for architecture —
the renewal of its language and
a new and deeper consciousness
of its relationship to social change.

Regardless of the indebted-
ness of Wright's architecture
to certain principles and
forms exhibited in nature, it
in no way presents an organic
totality. The Guggenheim presents a series of
contrasts: the building is radically alienated from
the urban fabric;

NAUTILUS SHELL, SECTION

administration block, gallery ramp, auditorium —
each functional unit is absolute, relating only to
itself; sweeping curve confronts sharp angle.

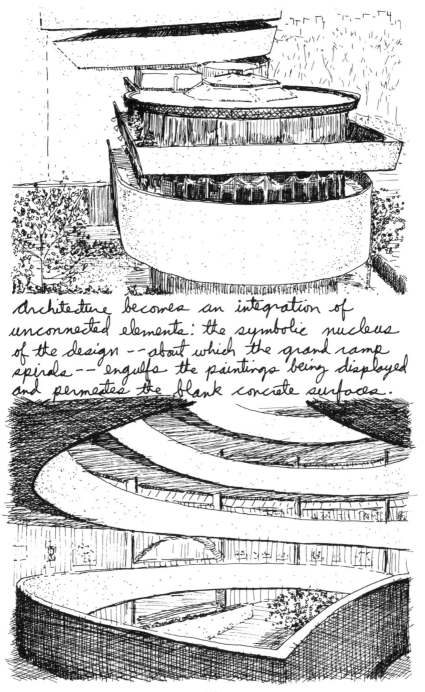

Architecture becomes an integration of unconnected elements: the symbolic nucleus of the design -- about which the grand ramp spirals -- engulfs the paintings being displayed and permeates the blank concrete surfaces.

GUGGENHEIM

It took a concerted effort to find a contracting firm willing to accept the challenge of building the guggenheim. The difficulties faced by the contractor and construction workers reflected the difficulties faced by the designer. The quarrel between expression and both function and construction remains unsettled. The very irreconcilability that emerges in the design _is_ its fundamental message.

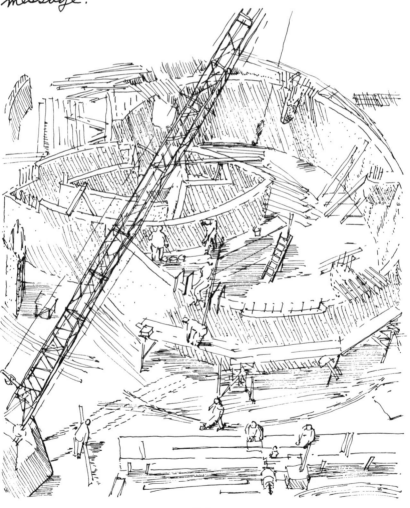

GUGGENHEIM

At the beginning of his career, Wright's task was analogous to that of a writer who must create a unique vocabulary and syntax for every sentence. He had to create a new language upon which he could rely. The more he perfected this self-made language, the more he was driven to perform daring

Guggenheim, 1948 design (above) -- 1949 design with office building (below).

architectural feats to justify his presumption --
exotic, overblown designs threatened to consume
his more substantial work. Maintaining the
delicate balance required by the demands
of his procedure, which at those moments in
his career when all seemed lost brought
him to the very edge of sanity, he had yet
another problem to confront -- the hostility
which greeted the results of his struggle.

Guggenheim, as built.

"If, viewed from the outside," one critic said
of the Guggenheim, "the building seems cramped,
its interior is marred in somewhat similar
fashion by a conflict between design and
function," and in the same petulant mood
concluded, "the good is mingled with the bad
most confusingly."

Another critic focused his attention on "the
famous ramp," which he found to be " a
lengthy parade, lacking intimacy and variety."

The whole museum thus became for him "a place to get through as quickly as possible."

"The building is a giant corkscrew."

"... a washing machine..."

"... a dictator's tomb..."

"The Guggenheim Museum is a building that should be put in a museum to show how mad the twentieth century is."

Perhaps the worst reaction came, not in hostile words, but in building designs that treated Wright's language as an architectural fad: Art Deco.

It would have been inexplicable if the beauty of the building materials and flowing space exposed in Wrights' work did not succeed in luring curious architects. It would have been even stranger if these architects had accepted the consequences. After all, Wright exposed not only the creative energy of modern architecture, but also the deception of that which preceded it in the culture and the work of these same architects. If they were attracted by the drama of Wrights' struggle, they were also fearful of the eruptive force that it represented. They may have been intrigued by the idea of freeing architecture, but in no way by the idea of freeing themselves. They translated Wrights' protest against their society and

137

profession into a fanciful memory of the past and dream image of the future. They viewed his architecture as they would a stylish outfit. If a design such as that for the Chrysler Building in New York City appears periodically in the architectural magazines, it is precisely because its modernity is so superficial. Art Deco fits the recurrent escapist and nostalgic mood in the United States all too well.

Even architects who were sympathetic with Wright's struggle and imitated his individualism developed symptoms of the same formalist infection. The number of Wright-inspired designs was never very high, and those which were built bear the marks, not only of being forced, but also of being played-out. None of Wright's

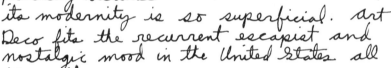

Section

Plan

NORMAN, OKLA.: Bavinger House (1950) Bruce Goff, designer.

138

followers succeeded in absorbing the contradiction evident in the relationship of a self-invented language to reality.

The contradiction was especially marked at the time the Guggenheim was being built. While the elaborate formwork of the grand ramp was being erected and its maze of reinforcing bars painstakingly threaded together, war-devastated Europe was being rebuilt with the use of newly developed methods of industrialized construction and in the United States rural communities were being transformed by procedures of mass production in the service of a profit-motivated building industry into Levittowns. In the light of these developments, the Guggenheim appeared uneconomical and indulgent on the one hand and idealistic on the other.

The extent of the contradiction becomes even clearer when an attempt is made to measure the Guggenheim according to the possibility of its being reproduced. A cartoon appeared at the time it was under construction that pictured a post-war suburban development with its curved streets lined, not with the typical box-like structure, but with Wright's famous "Falling Water house.

BEAR RUN, PA.: "Falling Water" House (1936).

Neither Falling Water nor the Guggenheim could be used as an aesthetic commodity in this way. Wright's concept of form was infused with too much tension. He grasped the contradictions of his art too firmly. The Guggenheim is a clenched fist.

SOURCES (in order of appearance in essay)

Summerson, John. *The Classical Language of Architecture*. Cambridge: M.I.T. Press, 1963.

Atkinson, R.J.C. *Stonehenge*. Harmondsworth, Middlesex: Penguin Books Ltd., 1960.

Bromehead, C.N. "Mining and Quarrying to the Seventeenth Century," *A History of Technology*. vol. 2. London: Oxford University Press, 1955.

Robertson, D.S. *Handbook of Greek and Roman Architecture*. London: Cambridge University Press, 1929.

Briggs, Martin S. "Building Construction," *A History of Technology*. vol. 2. London: Oxford University Press, 1955.

Murray, Peter. *Bramante's Tempietto*. Newcastle upon Tyne: University of Newcastle upon Tyne Press, 1972.

Hibbard, Howard. *Bernini*. Harmondsworth, Middlesex: Penguin Books Ltd., 1965.

Portoghesi, Paolo. *The Rome of Borromini*. New York: Braziller, 1968.

Lang, Jane. *Rebuilding St. Paul's*. London: Oxford University Press, 1956.

Downes, Kerry. *Hawksmoor*. New York: Praeger Publishers, 1969.

Sloane, Eric. *Museum of Early American Tools*. New York: Ballantine Books, 1964.

"Memorial Hall," *Yale Alumni Weekly* (New Haven, Connecticut), January 31, 1900.

Blake, Peter. "The Guggenheim: Museum or Monument," *Architectural Forum* (New York), December 1959.

Adorno, Theodor. *Prisms*. London: Neville Spearman Ltd., 1967.

PREFACE.

At the time I began work on this book, Joan and I were living in New Haven, Connecticut. We were part of a small group that met once a week to discuss the relationship between art and politics. In the course of these discussions we grappled with the concept of secular belief, how it was different from and similar to religious belief, and the manner in which belief is articulated in our time.

The Yale Center for British Art, designed by Louis Kahn, was nearing completion. Located on a major street in downtown New Haven, the project had been part of a long and bitter protest against expansion of the university in this area of the city. I had been watching the construction process with mixed feelings. As a political activist, I was troubled by Kahn's lack

After a drawing by Louis Kahn.

145

of response to the political, economic, and human conflicts involved. As an architect, I had gradually become aware of the power of Kahn's architecture. The design addressed the building's own demands with astonishing rigor and honesty. I began to understand what Kahn was trying to say when he wrote, "I recall the beginning as Belief."

I spelled out my questions about the building at one of our weekly meetings. The discussion that ensued suggested the guidelines of the analysis with which the following essay begins. In the course of this struggle with Kahn's thought, I periodically contemplated its relationship to religious belief. Two particular buildings invariably came to mind: Antonio Gaudi's Church of the Holy Family and Le Corbusier's Chapel at Ronchamps. Previously I had thought of Gaudi's handcrafted architecture as mystical and backward-looking,

After a drawing by Le Corbusier.

Le Corbusier's machine-age architecture as rational and addressed to the needs of the future. Now I suspected that this response was oversimplified. I began to look more closely at how and why these two buildings are such profound statements of religious and architectural belief in twentieth-century terms.

The contrast between idealist and realist thought was a critical issue in our

146

PREFACE

After a drawing by
Alvar Aalto.

art and politics group's
discussions of belief and
became the focus of the studies
that conclude this essay. The
idealist notions articulated in
Mies van der Rohe's design for
the campus of the Illinois
Institute of Technology are
examined, followed by an
analysis of the concept of
"communally binding realism"
articulated in Alvar Aalto's
design for a new civic center
in Helsinki.

YALE CENTER FOR BRITISH ART. New
Haven, Connecticut. Louis Kahn's last
architectural design. The exterior is flat
and grey. The grey of indifference:
indifference to the small New Haven stores,
offices, apartments, and studios that were
too easily removed to make room for it;

NEW HAVEN: View from corner of High and Chapel Streets (before).

indifference to the fact that Yale University -- not
the city -- got a private art collection in their
place; indifference to the workers who built the

148

building and will never again enter it (that worker I saw perched on a ladder sandpapering a concrete column by hand, inch by inch); indifference to the building's cost paid for in tax write-offs and in the life blood of Appalachia (the area exploited by the building's patron, the Mellon family; the area to which Yale has sent architectural students to design buildings in the "local architectural vernacular"). There are no windows, no balconies -- just grey steel, grey glass: the grey of Samuel Beckett's writing and Arnold Schoenberg's music, the grey of factory chimneys and city streets, the grey of the dehumanizing and self-perpetuating bureaucracy that follows in the wake of industrialization.

NEW HAVEN: View from corner of High and Chapel Streets (after).

The grey walls of Louis Kahn's design for the Yale Center for British Art do not present a pretty picture of the world, but by the same token they are not escapist and nostalgic like so much of the Yale campus -- with its "medieval" stonework, leaded windows opening onto sheltered courtyards, and bulldog scholars carved into hidden recesses, all built in the 1930's in the midst of the depression.

A New Haven worker recalls:

NEW HAVEN: Yale Law School.

Those stones are heavy. Each one of them was lifted into place by hand by someone desperate for a day's pay.

Every morning there was a shape-up. Yale was just about the only place in the city hiring. They could get all the workers they needed for a pittance.

At noon it was worse. The workers who had been taken on in the morning for some pitiful rate had to accept an even lower rate for the afternoon. Opposite the job site there would be a bunch of guys ready to take their place for just about no pay at all. We were all hungry for work.

Just as there is no nostalgia and escapism of the "medieval" variety in the grey walls of Louis Kahn's design, there are no "modern" tricks, such as those displayed in the walls of the nearby Art and Architecture Building, designed by

NEW HAVEN : Yale School of Art and Architecture (1963).

KAHN

Paul Rudolph, in
which floor slabs
seem to slide past
their supporting piers,
leaving us in
ignorance of the
way the building
is put together.

KAHN

Every detail of Kahn's design is rationally conceived, honestly articulated, and presented for us to see and assess.

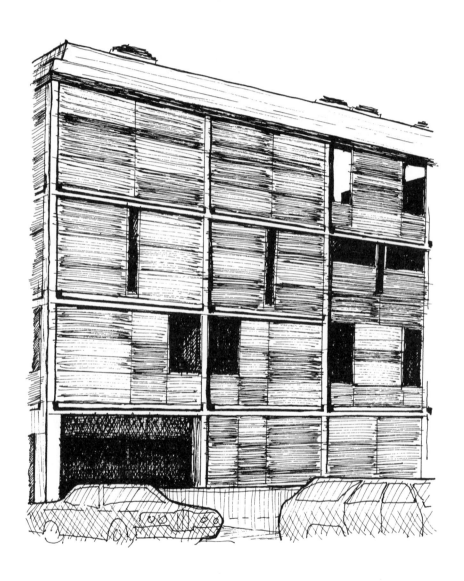

KAHN

The ground floor is three bays wide, five bays long. (A "bay" is the distance between structural columns.) This is one of many architectural quotations: 3 × 5, the "golden rectangle" of classical architecture.

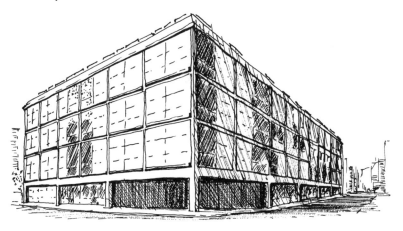

Such a quotation in this context is a gesture, a reaching out -- for above all else the flat grey walls of this design speak of loneliness, the loneliness of those who are isolated in the cars that press together bumper-to-bumper on the streets of the city.

Kahn brought the columns which form the structural bays to the edge of the sidewalk and allocated the space between them to specialty shops.

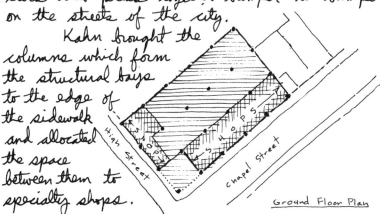

Ground Floor Plan

View into sunken courtyard.

Nevertheless, the art gallery and shops remain in separate worlds; there are no connecting doors. If anything, the shops increase the distance between the gallery and the life of the street. Similarly, the taxes paid by the shops, only a fraction of the taxes paid by the site's previous occupants, underline the problem that Yale's tax exempt status creates for the city.

In the 1940's Louis Kahn wrote pamphlets with Oscar Stonorov, who was killed along with Walter Reuther, then president of the CIO, when Reuther's plane mysteriously exploded in 1970. The pamphlets were titled, "Why

City Planning Is Your Responsibility" and "You and Your Neighborhood." However, when Kahn got a commission in the 1960's to develop a plan for

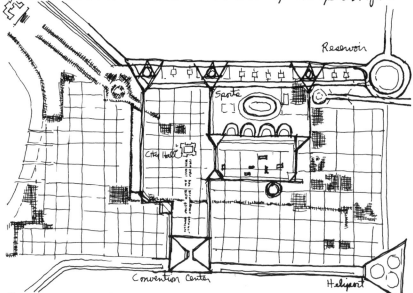

PROJECT: Philadelphia, Market Street East Renewal Plan, 1961.

the Hill neighborhood of New Haven, he could not cope with the demand of the people in the neighborhood to participate in the planning process. He eventually dropped the commission as he was prone to do when the situation was not right for his art.

Order is intangible
It is a level of creative consciousness
    forever becoming higher in level
The higher the order the more diversity in design
Order supports integration
From what space wants to be the unfamiliar
    may be revealed to the architect.
From order he will derive creative force
    and power of self-criticism to give
    form to this unfamiliar.
Beauty will evolve. (Louis Kahn, 1955)

157

Kahn lost the last remnant of his plan for the Hill neighborhood posthumously when the lowest construction bid for his design for the Hill Central School came in nearly 40% above the budget. There was no connection between his precise art and his vague political conscience.

On the upper floors of the Yale Center for British Art the structural bay is divided in half -- the 40 - foot bay divided into two 20 - foot bays -- and the theme of the infill panel is introduced ("infill panel" is the surface between structural columns). This design theme is another quotation: the framing pattern of the traditional Japanese house. The theme is then varied from panel to panel...

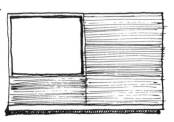

design theme

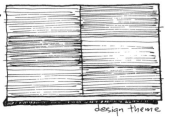

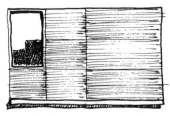

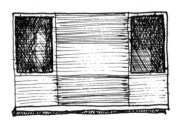

The variations are organized in such a way that there appears to be an absolute need for each and each seems to fulfill a precise function. Their juxtaposition determines the composition...

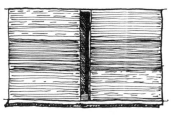

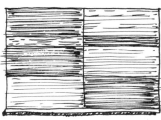

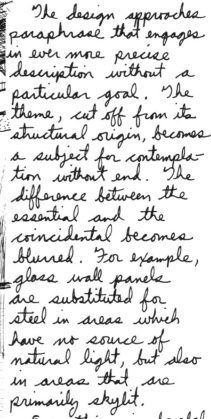

The design approaches paraphrase that engages in ever more precise description without a particular goal. The theme, cut off from its structural origin, becomes a subject for contemplation without end. The difference between the essential and the coincidental becomes blurred. For example, glass wall panels are substituted for steel in areas which have no source of natural light, but also in areas that are primarily skylit.

Everything is absorbed into variation. Design, as such, is brought to a standstill. The architecture is utterly static. It utterly dominates nature. It represents a longing, present in architecture since the first boulder was upended to make the first column, to reduce reality to an orderly system -- a

KAHN

View from Art and Architecture Building. At left is Yale Art Gallery designed by Louis Kahn, 1953.

longing which has been intensified by modern industry's capacity to mechanically reproduce entire building systems.

The architect's voice is heard both despite and by means of his design technique. By means of it because architecture becomes capable of restraining itself coldly and inexorably, which is the only position for architecture since the development of industrialized building. The most unconvincing features of a modern architectural design are those most clearly ornamental, the concrete fins on the top floor of Rudolph's Art and Architecture Building, for example.

Louis Kahn's voice can be heard

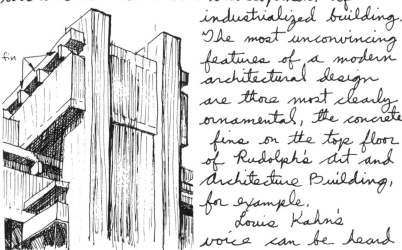

fin

Art and Architecture Building.

despite his design technique because the spirit which thought out an unrelentingly grey architecture remains sufficiently in control to repeatedly penetrate the building's technical components and bring them to life. Kahn neither passively resigned himself to the dictates of the building industry nor belligerently turned his back on them. He worked with the construction materials and techniques of his time, and in so doing, developed a new mechanical system, a new finish for the steel wall panels, a new method of skylighting.

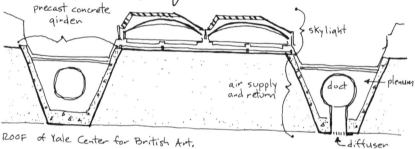

precast concrete girder

skylight

air supply and return

duct

plenum

diffuser

ROOF of Yale Center for British Art.

The roof is composed of upraised concrete arms which support a continuous skylighting system. Frank Lloyd Wright's design for the Guggenheim Museum, also created in the final years of the architect's life, comes to mind. In both Kahn's design and Wright's the wall turns away from the street; in both, a hollow interior

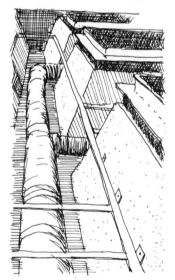

turns to the sky with a gesture that seems
charged with allegorical force. But Wright's
skylight confronts the heavens openly and
directly, while Kahn's skylights are guarded
with metal louvers above and plastic, light—

diffusing panels below. Wright utilized industrial technology to open the interior of his design to sunlight. Kahn utilized industrial technology to open the roof of the Yale Center for British Art, but at the same time to protect the interior from the direct rays of the sun (and to block out north light altogether).

In Kahn's design the expression of tension, contradiction, and pain is unrelieved; it takes on fixed contours and becomes material. Columns, wall panels, floor slabs, and roof are not the media of personal resolution, but

by no means do they
deny their origin:
"I recall the beginning
as Belief," Louis Kahn
said.

The architectural
elements become
characters of objective
protest. The gesture
of the roof is charged
with all that is denied
in the design of the
walls: stress and
direction, the image
of eruption, the
gesture of a stifled
cry. The design
comes to master the
suffering it proclaims.
The roof is a sign,
a signal, a message
of survival -- of
despair but not defeat.

The interior is
surfaced with white oak,
beige linen and carpeting.
The master of one of
Yale's residential colleges
upon concluding a tour
of the building said,
"I find the exterior un-
bearable, but the interior
quite beautiful. There is
a contradiction here."

KAHN

The core of the design for the interior is an enclosed stair located as far as possible from the exterior. It is a concrete cylinder with its own roof that, like the roof of the building, is transparent yet inward turning. It is a miniature structure within the larger structure, an interior within the interior.

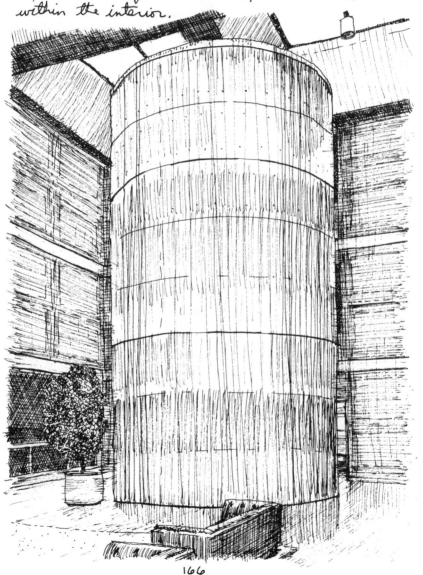

KAHN

The detailing of the stair, especially its stainless steel handrail, is meticulous. The call for symmetry urgently voiced by the design is inexorably denied by the door at each floor -- just as the urge for symmetry of the building is denied by the corner location of the main entrance. The stairwell is peaceful and very beautiful, but it is impossible to linger here. It is a stair and therefore demands movement.

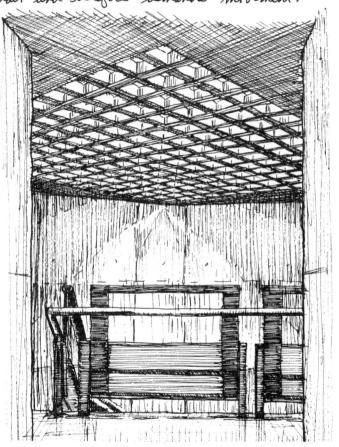

Kahn's design for the Yale Center for British Art represents the truth of an architect who recognized the untruth of his society and, at

the same time, was part of that untruth.
Without the revolutionary optimism of Frank
Lloyd Wright's Guggenheim Museum, without
its passion, but perhaps more in keeping
with the struggle before us, the design
offers the image of art restrained but
still possible.

THE CHAPEL AT RONCHAMP, designed by Le Corbusier and built in the mid-1950's, is located in a rural part of France at the top of a tree-covered hill. The floor of the chapel follows the natural slope of the site down to the altar. The floor is constructed of smooth, poured-in-place concrete except at the altars where it is native stone. The

View towards main altar.

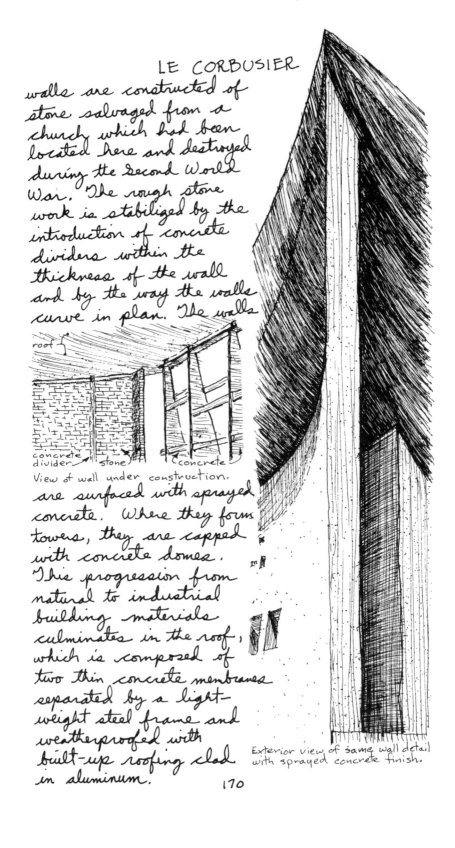

walls are constructed of
stone salvaged from a
church which had been
located here and destroyed
during the Second World
War. The rough stone
work is stabilized by the
introduction of concrete
dividers within the
thickness of the wall
and by the way the walls
curve in plan. The walls

roof

concrete
divider   stone   concrete

View of wall under construction.

are surfaced with sprayed
concrete. Where they form
towers, they are capped
with concrete domes.
This progression from
natural to industrial
building materials
culminates in the roof,
which is composed of
two thin concrete membranes
separated by a light-
weight steel frame and
weatherproofed with
built-up roofing clad
in aluminum.

Exterior view of same wall detail
with sprayed concrete finish.

170

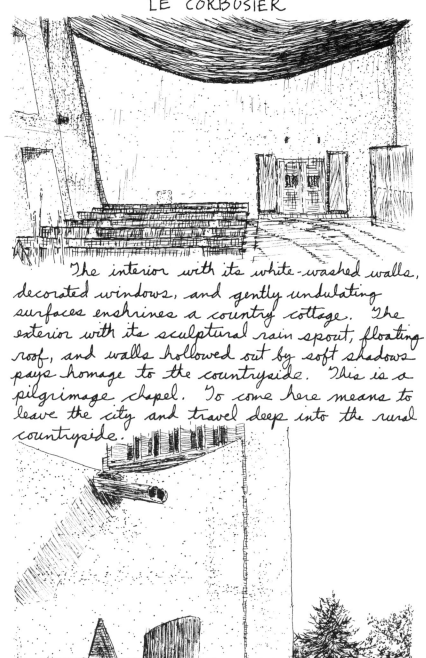

The interior with its white-washed walls, decorated windows, and gently undulating surfaces enshrines a country cottage. The exterior with its sculptural rain spout, floating roof, and walls hollowed out by soft shadows pays homage to the countryside. This is a pilgrimage chapel. To come here means to leave the city and travel deep into the rural countryside.

LE CORBUSIER

When Le Corbusier wrote Towards a New Architecture in the early 1920's, he believed that the purpose of modern architecture was to replace the landscape of the past, with its reliance upon isolated farming families, with the communal ideals of a working-class-based industrial society. The building unit of the new landscape would not be the isolated cottage, but a neighborhood in which dwellings would be designed in the context of day-care, medical, educational, recreational, and administrative facilities, and within easy reach of both agriculture and industry.

Seine   Île de la Cité

PROJECT: Plan "Voisin" for Paris (1922-30).

LE CORBUSIER

In the 1920's Le Corbusier directed a generation of architects towards functional details, the flat roof, plain wall, and flush horizontal window. Thirty years later he pointed towards an architecture of sculptural details, irregular silhouette, rough concrete surfaces, and deep-sunk openings in both wall and roof. In place

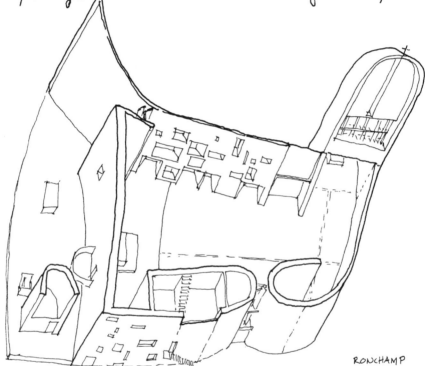

RONCHAMP

of his earlier aesthetic, which had been inspired by the precision of machine technology, Le Corbusier substituted a freehand quality, turning to nature and rural building forms for inspiration. At the same time, however, he continued to be inspired by new building materials and techniques.

LE CORBUSIER

There are antagonists within the structure at Ronchamp. Modern materials and industrial design push towards the future. The rural setting, traditional building materials, and the function of the chapel lean towards the past. It is not only these antagonists who are there, but the architect as well, struggling to reconcile the contending forces within the confines of his art.

CHURCH OF THE HOLY FAMILY. Barcelona.

In the early 1920's, at the same time Le Corbusier was writing Towards a New Architecture, Antonio Gaudí's "Cathedral of the Poor" was being built. Gaudí lived on the site and developed the details of the design by talking them out with the people doing the work. After his death in 1926, work on the building was continued, at first with money and labor donated by the people of Barcelona, later by people from around the world. What explains the relevance of a design and building method that seem so out of step with their own time -- that is, the 1920's addressed by Le Corbusier's book --

BARCELONA: Church of the Holy Family (1883-1926).

175

GAUDÍ

and even more out of
step with our time of
computer design and
mass-produced building
components?

gaudí's early work,
the buildings he designed
in the 1870's and 1880's,
reveal truly imaginative
engineering, inventive
use of the currently
fashionable architectural
styles, a deep knowledge
and love of local building
materials and crafts.

He designed a large
suburban villa, three
city mansions, a modest
college building, a
warehouse, pavilions
for a trade exhibit. In
1884 he was made
director of works for
a large Neo-Gothic
church on which
construction had begun
two years earlier. By
1893, he had completed
the crypt and a small
portion of the outer walls
according to the original
design, which by the
standards of its time was
quite conventional.

COMILLAS: El Capricho (1883-85).

GAUDÍ

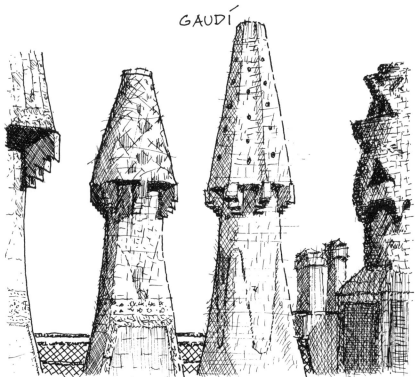

BARCELONA: Güell House (1885-89), chimneys on the roof.

Gaudí's inspiration, as for many of his contemporaries in Europe and the United States, originated in the medieval past, and that past in Spain included the Moorish architectural tradition. Much of the detailing in his early work, which might appear original and exotic to non-Spanish eyes -- such as floral tiling, sculpturesque chimney-pots, elaborate woodwork, and wrought iron grillwork -- was based on local precedents and building traditions. Gaudí was, first and last, an architect of his place and time: Barcelona at the turn of the century.

An architect is a person who stands before a work table with eyes fixed upon a certain image. What is being looked at so intently is something that is not one object but innumerable objects. Even the simplest building deals with more than one set of problems, with more than one period of time. A column begins at a plane, rises through space, receives a structural load; it forms a dot

SANTA COLOMA DE CERVELLO: Colonia Güell chapel (1898-1914).

in space or, in association with other columns, divides one space from another; it makes a cultural reference. What an architect looks at is something that changes -- life-- and an architect looks at it in a special way.

GAUDÍ

Gaudí was a religious architect, perhaps the most deeply religious architect of our time. He was also a deeply political architect. He called the church to which he devoted over forty years of his working life "cathedral of the poor." During the last years of his life, he lived in a small workshop next to the church, his bed surrounded by books, plaster casts, and structural study models.

"As my body weakens," he would say, "my spirit feels more agile and free." Every afternoon he would take a walk -- generally to the church of St. Philip Neri. On one of these afternoon walks he was knocked down by a trolley car. Because of his humble appearance, he was taken to the charity ward of a nearby hospital. Three days later he was dead! From all over Barcelona people came -- intellectual workers, people who worked with their hands, friends, people of his parish -- and brought Gaudí back to his cathedral of the poor, where he was buried.

It was the column upon which Gaudí focused his attention. He explained that "the architecture of the Renaissance condemned the deception of the gothic structural system [in which interior columns require exterior buttressing] and the modern builder should condemn it also."

After a drawing by Gaudí.

179

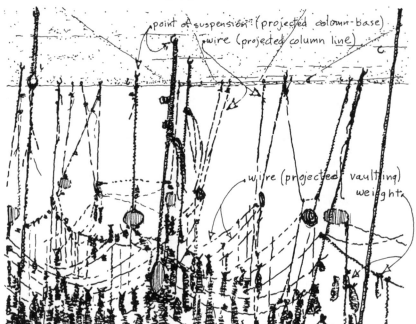

Partial view of structural model. The points of suspension in the model correspond to the bases of columns in the projected structure.

He studied the loads and stresses produced by the gothic roofing system, erecting a series of wires with attached weights. Each weight represented the load which the building element represented by the wire would have to support. The wires then described the actual structural lines of the building. This procedure produced the tilted column, which became the defining feature of Gaudí's "modern gothic" architecture.

He next studied the shape of the column—round, square, polygonal, star-shaped—and the way the column branched out to

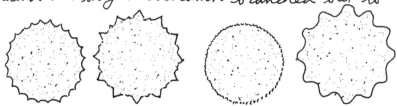

Cross section of the nave.

GAUDÍ

receive the structural load.
Again he made many study
models and as always
turned to the principles
of nature for inspiration
and guidance. After
determining the center
of gravity of each
section of the main
roof, he directed the
top of the column
towards it. He then
allowed the column
to branch out to
support a section of
the side aisle roof
or balcony floor.
The center of gravity
of the whole determined
the tilt of the lower
part of the column,
which eliminated the
need for the buttressing
and construction
scaffolding used in the
gothic system. Gaudí's
final studies of the
column concerned the
play of light and
shadow on various
surface patterns,
which he altered from
lower column to
structural branches to
upper column.

During the course of his life's work, Gaudí tended to develop forms that were more and more sculptural; forms that suggest more and more insistently the use of concrete, a material readily available to him and one that lends itself to being molded. Yet he continued to use stone and brick, the building materials with which the medieval cathedrals were built. We can not be certain of what Gaudí may have accomplished had he adopted the newer building materials and techniques, but we can be certain that the beliefs he articulated in his design for the Church of the Holy Family continue to address pressing architectural and political concerns. He believed in creating a gathering place for the poor, having the workers who built the building participate in the design process, finding

BARCELONA: Milà house (1905-10)

182

construction techniques that suited the expression of the building and the skills of workers using hand-operated tools.

Even today, Gaudí's design and construction methods are generally considered mystical and backward-looking while Le Corbusier's are regarded as rational and technologically progressive. More relevant in assessing these architects is the struggle for belief underlying their work, for it constitutes the intention and is the formative principle of their architecture. The same wind that blows through the lacy towers of Gaudí's cathedral of the poor catches the billowing roof of Le Corbusier's pilgrimage chapel; the same force propels both designs from a deeply understood past to a visionary but problematic future.

After a drawing by Mies van der Rohe.

ILLINOIS INSTITUTE OF TECHNOLOGY (IIT), designed by Mies van der Rohe. In isolation, a detail may be a genuine enough reflection of some piece of the reality of a given building. Whether or not the sequence and organization of details reflect anything beyond this level of reality depends on the architect's attitude towards reality as a whole. It is this attitude which determines the importance that the individual detail is accorded in the context of the design as a whole. If handled uncritically --that is, if there is no distinction between significant and irrelevant detail, architecture becomes, at best, factual reporting; more usually, it remains utterly silent.

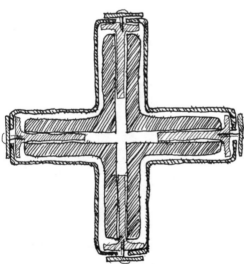

BARCELONA: German Pavilion (1928-29), plan view of column.

How does the architect establish criteria by which details are selected--

184

that is, how is the principle of selection formed? Mies van der Rohe, speaking for many architects of his generation, answered with an aphorism: Less is More, which might be interpreted: architecture is the subtraction of the inessential. But what is the subjective principle guiding Mies' process of subtraction? What is the relationship between objective building requirements and the recurring details which are the signature of his architecture -- such as curtain walls with regularly spaced protruding I-beams, highly articulated corners, and crisply defined infill panels? Clearly there is a divergence between objective requirements and subjective decisions in Mies' work. For example, in designing the curtain wall for the Seagram Building, Mies denied the physical and psychological need

CHICAGO: IIT, Crown Hall (1950-56).

of the building's users to operate window sash, adjust window shading, and control ceiling lighting. However, it would be wrong to think of his architecture as anti-functional, just as it would be wrong to think of his architecture as anti-historical. There was in Mies' work an ongoing battle between program and design -- between past, present, and future -- no less than there was in the work of Gaudí and Le Corbusier.

Mies was born in 1884 in Aachen, which had been the seat of the Holy Roman Empire and where from the ninth to the sixteenth centuries most of the German kings were crowned. He was educated in the Cathedral School of Aachen under the influence of the teaching of Thomas Aquinas and in the haunting presence of Charlemagne, whose remains have lain buried in the cathedral crypt since 804 and

AACHEN: imperial church (796-804).

whose throne still stands in the gallery. Mies died in 1969 in Chicago, where his influence as a designer and educator established "Miesian" as a sub-style of modern architecture.

Neither his life nor his architecture was constant or static. Each was a process, a movement alternating now away from, now towards, subjective memories of the past and objective realities of the present. It was the act of subtraction Mies undertook in his work that constituted the link between his inner life and the outside world -- a link not easily made and once made not casually altered. The concreteness of Mies' thought enabled him to produce an architecture that was formally consistent and convincing. This was the source of its suggestive power and vitality. Mies' detailing was no stylistic device. It was part and parcel of the

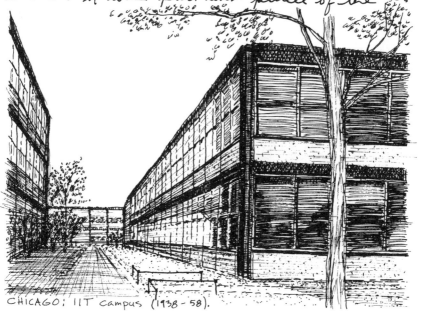

CHICAGO; IIT Campus (1938-58).

aesthetic ambition informing his work both as
designer and educator.

For Mies the tie to the architecture of
the past was hardly equivalent to a simple
sequence of buildings. It was an idea
alternately recalled and repressed in the
history of architecture; classicism. Mies
thought through the idea of classicism to

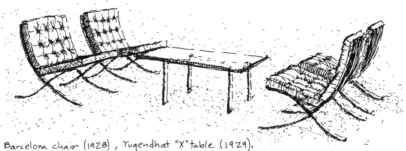

Barcelona chair (1928), Tugendhat "X" table (1929).

its conclusion. What was crucial in the design
of the classical facade was not its details
as such, but rather the specific function
the details assumed in the presentation
of the underlying structure of the
architectural concept. Mies disposed
of the facade and slowly, through
the gradual refinement of detail, made
that underlying structure visible and
articulate. In so doing, he became
heir to the classical tradition. The
spirit of classicism was far more
present in his work than in that of any
of his contemporaries who deliberately
set out to be classical (especially those
who did so tongue in cheek).

In a speech made in 1960 on the

occasion of receiving the Gold Medal of the American Institute of architects Mies ironically commented that it was not necessary nor possible to invent a new kind of architecture every Monday morning. He observed that architecture can be an expression of the innermost structure of its time, and argued:

> This is the structure from which architecture emerges. It follows, then, that architecture should be related to only the most significant forces in the civilization. Only a relationship which touches the essence of the time can be real. This relation I like to call a truth relation. Truth in the sense of Thomas Aquinas, as the adaequatio intellectus et rei. Or, as a modern philosopher expresses it in the language of today: truth is the significance of facts. Only such a relation is able to embrace the complex nature of civilization. And only so, will it express the slow unfolding of its form.

The compulsion to purge architecture of chance and arbitrariness led Mies not only to new details, but also to a new expressive dimension of site planning. His image for the campus plan and relationships between the numerous buildings he designed for IIT between 1942 and 1957 was that of a winter landscape in the

Great Plains: cool, distant, resistant to any tendency to ingratiate itself with the viewer -- that is, resistant to personal identification and empathy.

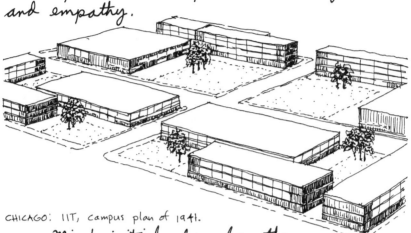

CHICAGO: IIT, campus plan of 1941.

Mies' initial plan for the eight square city blocks of the proposed campus placed several large paired buildings symmetrically on either side of a central axis. In his second plan of 1941 he imposed the additional discipline of the double-square proportional system of classical architecture on the development of the campus, dividing it into a grid of structural modules that were each 24 feet wide, 24 feet deep, and 12 feet high. This grid determined the horizontal and vertical dimensions of the buildings both internally and externally as well as their placement on the site. Within a particular building there might be any number of functions with quite specific and different requirements -- lecture halls, workshops, laboratories, seminar rooms, faculty offices, storage areas, and washrooms. The structural

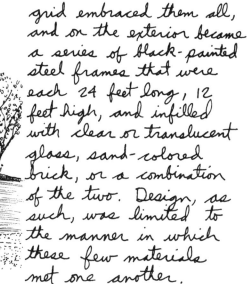

grid embraced them all, and on the exterior became a series of black-painted steel frames that were each 24 feet long, 12 feet high, and infilled with clear or translucent glass, sand-colored brick, or a combination of the two. Design, as such, was limited to the manner in which these few materials met one another.

In his final placement of individual buildings on the site Mies made every effort to negate perspective and the feeling of spatial depth. He overlapped the buildings in such a manner that beyond each structure another one would visually slide out from the one in front as the viewer moved towards it, closing the visual gap and setting up a visual movement that would neutralize the physical movement. Mies did not abolish space; rather he underlined it — that is, he made it something peculiarly architectural. He dissociated the feeling

of progress from that of movement and demanded
that we give to each moment, each detail our
full attention. Metals research, alumni
memorial, metallurgical and chemical engineering,
chemistry, boiler plant, gas technology,
administration, mechanical engineering, chapel,
architecture and design, dormitories, commons,
railroad laboratory, electrical engineering, and
physics... there is no hierarchy of building
forms, no spatial development. The resolution
of each detail is equal in stature to that
of the architecture as a whole.

"The long path from material through
function to creative work has one goal: to
create order out of the desperate confusion
of our time," Mies said at the conclusion
of his inaugural address at IIT (then
the Armour Institute). "We must have
order, allocating to each thing its proper

place and giving to each thing its due according to its nature."

Mies had excluded the ornamental material of the classical language of architecture and purged its structural categories of their aesthetic implications. Yet he continued to speak the idiom and strive for the kind of architectural order which was inseparably tied to what he had eliminated. The contradiction hindered Mies' further development as much as it focused it, and was partly responsible for the tension inherent in his work. The pull in Mies' work between a developmental view of architecture on the one hand and a static view on the other was necessarily great and essentially unresolvable; the more he adjusted the focus, the more the tension increased. Mies did not design buildings on a campus for IIT, rather he designed a paradigm for an architecture that is not: isolated shapes, shadowless surfaces, structural forces without motion, architectural gestures paralyzed.

THE ARCHITECT'S VIEW of human existence--
more precisely, of human potentiality, has
specific architectural implications. The architecture
that comes to mind when Le Corbusier's work
in the early 1920's is mentioned or the work
done at the Bauhaus under the leadership
of Gropius in the late 1920's and Mies
van der Rohe in the early 1930's is an
architecture that avoids exaggerated
proportions, unneccesarily complex connections,
and false relationships! It is an architecture

DESSAU: Bauhaus (1925-26), designed by Walter Gropius.

that does not construct hybrid spectacles. It
does not work as an accumulation of signs
borrowed from the past or as a proliferation
of experimental building techniques. It avoids
everything that would make of either design
or the building process something more than
it is. It is an architecture that denies us
the comfort of daydreaming about either the
past or the future. It forces us to confront
the limitations imposed on us by the
present. It is life as it really is -- in any
case, that is the idea that comes to mind
in recalling early modern architecture.

But in life potentiality can become
reality. Political developments before, during,
and after the Second World War created a

GROPIUS

BALTIMORE: Temple Oheb Shalom (1957), designed by Gropius with TAC.

situation in which Le Corbusier, Gropius, and Mies, among millions of other people, were confronted with the necessity of making choices that fundamentally altered the direction of their lives. Of course, the situation was extreme, but the change in their work as designers, educators, and thinkers, in each case quite different, could never have been predicted.

TIME AND CHANGE:
rain running down and
scoring the face of rock;
stone slowly breaking,
dissolving, becoming soil;
soil working its way down
hillsides towards the
curving edges of lakes,
rivers, and the sea; the
land's edge worn away
by the movement of water.

In the course of
Alvar Aalto's life Finland
went through a basic
transformation. It shaped
and, in turn, was partly
shaped by his architecture.
At the time of Aalto's birth
in 1898 Finland had
partial autonomy within
the Russian empire as a
dukedom with its own
constitution. The imperial
reins were being tightened,
however, and consequently
agitation for Finnish
independence was
increasing. Some
constitutional concessions
were won during the
Russian revolutionary
outbreaks of 1905, but
the imperial grip soon
tightened again.

AALTO

I was born into a family of engineers. When I was a child, the place where I played was under my father's desk, the big white table. Difficult problems were solved there, with the aid of map readings. These solutions were influenced not only by practical considerations but also by more far-reaching aims. In order to do the job in a satisfactory way what was needed was a "communally binding realism." And it has been a realistic approach that has for the most part inspired my imagination. (An excerpt from an interview with Aalto recorded in 1972.)

Finland finally won full independence with the Russian revolution of 1917, and a Finnish Workers Socialist government was proclaimed. It was overthrown by an ex-general from the Russian imperial army who raised an army of White guards, which included 12,000 troops from Germany, who subsequently invited a German prince to be king. The scheme collapsed along with the German monarchy, and a democratic, parliamentary government was established.

Our time is full of enthusiasm for and interest in architecture because of the architectural revolution which is taking place during these last decades, but it is like all revolutions: it starts with enthusiasm and it stops with some sort of dictatorship. It runs off the track... (An excerpt from a talk given by Aalto in 1957.)

The young democracy was soon dominated by the fascist Lapua movement, and in the 1930's Aalto's country drifted into the orbit of Germany. When Hitler attacked the Soviet Union in 1941, Finland was his ally.

Aalto spent 1940 teaching in the United States and beginning his research on town planning and post-war reconstruction that was to remain the focus of his attention throughout the Second World War. The German army, before being driven out of Finland, devastated the northern part of the country. In 1945 Aalto delivered two talks on reconstruction of that area and began work on an urban design project for the town of Rovaniemi, which was not completed until 1975.

> There is one good thing that we still have today... well organized groups of creative people calling themselves architects, with a new real -- what should I say? -- direction for the world. Slowly, from being formal artists, they haved moved over into a new field; today they are the new garde d'honneur, the hard-fighting squadron for humanist technique in our time. (Continuation of the excerpt quoted above.)

Aiming at a truthful reflection of reality, Aalto's work focused on potentiality, both concrete and abstract:

> Today we must face the necessity of finding a system that will help the growth of our cities keep step with potential

supplies. In the same way every detail of reconstruction, ideological as well as material, must evolve organically. We must build houses that will grow.

The growing house should replace the "machine to live in" [which Le Corbusier had postulated in Towards a New Architecture]. This is the human approach for the builder today.

HELSINKI; architect's studio (1953–56).

It was in the complex tissue of architecture's interaction with environment that Aalto found the principle that enabled him to distinguish concrete potentiality from the infinity of purely abstract potentialities. In 1947 he wrote about a particular design as follows:

I spent a great deal of time making children's drawings, representing an imaginary mountain, with different shapes on the slopes and a sort of celestial superstructure consisting of several suns, which shed an equal light on the sides of the mountain. In themselves these drawings had nothing to do with architecture, but from these drawings

sprang a combination of plans and sections
which, although it would be difficult to
describe how, were all interwoven. And
this became the idea of the Municipal
Library [Viipuri, 1927-35]... the reading
rooms and the lending rooms on different
levels, like on the slope of a mountain,
around a central control desk uppermost
in the building. Above everything was
erected a sort of solar system -- the
round conical skylights.

The initial drawings of an imaginary
landscape, which belonged wholly to the
realm of subjectivity, had, in Aalto's words,
nothing to do with architecture. What
concerned him was the relationship between
his imagined shapes and suns and
objective reality. Aalto perceived reality
not only in terms of immediate requirements,
such as the need for natural light, reading
and lending rooms, and a control desk,
but also in terms of the requirements
of particular building materials, which he
saw projected from the shadows of the past.
In an article written in 1969 on the
relationship between architecture, painting,
and sculpture he said:

It is not through simple sketches
and superficial similarities in shape
that [the three art forms] influence
each other, but through "materia": an
intellectual analysis of the chosen material...
The materials that the three arts
use to make their statement have already

MUURATSALO: architect's house (1953).

been in existence for millenia. They are
as old as human culture itself, if not
older...

It is wood, the natural material,
which is the closest to [us], both
biologically and also as the environment
of original forms of culture...

Stone is also a natural product,
only much older still than the trees
growing around us...

Metal alloys are younger materials
discovered through ... technical
skills, but which, nevertheless, have a
shape in the "status nascendi".

AALTO

Every year new synthetic materials are being produced in semi-industrial and industrial fields. But "materia" requires time, and not all of the new materials are mature enough to be used fully for human purposes...

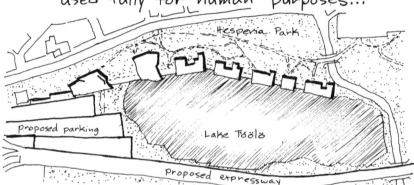

HELSINKI: New Center, 2nd project (1961-64).

Between 1959 and 1973 Aalto designed and periodically revised a plan for a new civic center for Helsinki. He also designed and supervised construction of the first of a series of public facilities proposed for the new center, "Finlandia" Concert and Congress Hall, between 1962 and 1975, the year before his death.

At the time the Czars ruled in Russia, Helsinki's old city center symbolized Finland's partial autonomy. Aalto felt the urban center of an independent Finland with democratic political aspirations demanded new relationships and new solutions, which he viewed as the task of his generation. After a series of studies, he concluded that the old center should be preserved and restored as a monument to earlier political struggles and that

202

the new center should be located at the nexus of two major traffic arteries and the main railroad station adjacent to the Parliament Building. His attitude towards the design of the existing park and lake was consistent with his concept of communally binding realism; it was "sentimentally preserved landscaping, but not in a satisfactory solution." To Aalto it seemed "rather comical to set in the midst of the heavily built-up urban center the unfortunate copy of a Karelian forest lake" (Alvar Aalto, Volume 2).

He sliced an expressway along one bank of the lake, lined the opposite bank with a series of public buildings, and ran a paved walkway along the edge of the lake beneath the buildings. At the end of the lake where the two circulation systems met he splayed a series of paved roof terraces of a parking garage into the lake.

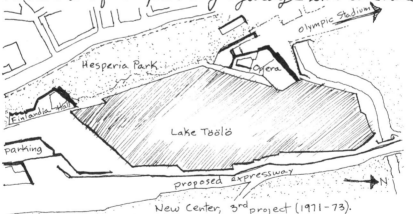

New Center, 3rd project (1971-73).

In his third design for the project ten years later Aalto extended the paved walkway around the opposite end of the lake, jutted the proposed opera house out into the lake, and branched an extension of the walkway from the opera house north towards the existing sports stadium and trades fair building. He also removed the last traces of the original shoreline. Despite all the proposed construction, however, Aalto not only preserved the planted area of the existing park but slightly expanded it. In the new civic center, rock, soil, and water would be perceived in an industrialized context.

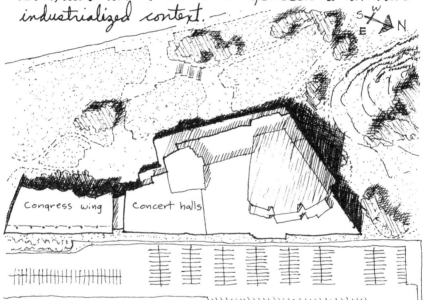

HELSINKI: "Finlandia" Concert and Congress Hall (1962-75) site plan.

The details of Aalto's design for "Finlandia" Hall encourage the building's users to wander, contemplate alternatives, and make choices. Each of the four elevations is oriented and responsive to a different situation. The east elevation extends in a straight line along the side of the proposed parking terraces and provides vehicular entrances to the congress wing,

AALTO

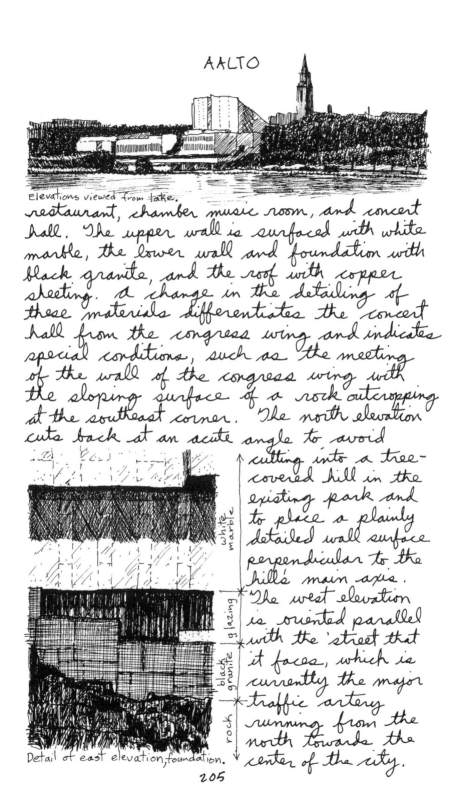

Elevations viewed from lake.

restaurant, chamber music room, and concert hall. The upper wall is surfaced with white marble, the lower wall and foundation with black granite, and the roof with copper sheeting. A change in the detailing of these materials differentiates the concert hall from the congress wing and indicates special conditions, such as the meeting of the wall of the congress wing with the sloping surface of a rock outcropping at the southeast corner. The north elevation cuts back at an acute angle to avoid cutting into a tree-covered hill in the existing park and to place a plainly detailed wall surface perpendicular to the hill's main axis. The west elevation is oriented parallel with the street that it faces, which is currently the major traffic artery running from the north towards the center of the city.

white marble

glazing

black granite

rock

Detail of east elevation, foundation.

Detail of west elevation, upper portion of wall.

At the juncture of the concert hall and congress wing the straight line gives way to a series of arcs that gradually shift towards a line running parallel with the east elevation. This highly articulated elevation provides pedestrian entrances from the park to each of the facilities within the building. The short south elevation is set at a right angle to the last of the series of arcs that form the west wall of the congress wing and, together with the north elevation, inclines towards the joining of the two wings of the building.

Each elevation is placed in a specific context; the significance of each detail, its functional meaning, is carefully defined. The interior and exterior space of the building, its structure and detailing, are all firmly rooted in a particular topographical, technological, social, and historical situation, free from transcendental reference.

Elevations viewed from the park.

The practical purpose of the given building constitutes for me the intuitive point of departure, the realism, which is my guiding principle [Alvar Aalto, Volume 3].

Each face of the congress wing, each section of the concert hall is comprised of carefully detailed resolutions of clearly defined problems. This is the source of the building's odd configuration and rich variety of details. However, definition never becomes an end in itself; the design never lapses into functionalism.

In looking at a floor plan of "Finlandia" Hall, the enclosing wall seems to wander in a narrow line past a peaceful park and then past the city's major transit facilities with pauses here and there for an entrance or a bridged gap; with rises, drops, and twists; odd contacts with the natural features of the site; glimpses into the interior; and from under the brow of the arcade,

207

views outward of a church tower and the Parliament Building.

Each detail of the civic center design is significant to the extent that it expresses the dialectic between person as individual and person as social being in a land of countless lakes and endless forests that is being transformed into a modern industrial nation. It is the tensions and contradictions within the individual and underlying the individual's relation with nature and with other human beings in a changing society that molded the design of "Finlandia" Hall. It is Aalto's belief that these tensions and contradictions could be resolved by a communally binding realism that is the source of the design's evocative power and harmony of proportions.

SOURCES

Aalto, E. and Fleig, K. (eds.). *Alvar Aalto*. Vol. III.
  Zurich: Verlag für Architektur Artemis, 1978.

Adorno, Theodor. *Philosophy of Modern Music*.
  New York: Seabury Press, 1973.

Berger, John. *Success and Failure of Picasso*.
  Baltimore: Penguin Books, 1965.

Benjamin, Walter. *Illuminations*. New York:
  Schocken Books, 1969.

Caudwell, Christopher. *Illusion and Reality*.
  New York: International Publishers, 1937.

Fischer, Ernst. *Art Against Ideology*.
  London: Penguin Books, 1969.

Le Corbusier 1952-1957. Zurich: Editions
  Girsberger, 1957.

Lukács, Georg, *Realism In Our Time*.
  New York: Harper Torchbooks, 1971.

Marx, Karl. *Economic and Philosophic
  Manuscripts* of 1844. New York:
  International Publishers, 1964.

Speyer, A. James. *Mies van der Rohe*.
  Chicago: Art Institute of Chicago, 1968.

Sweeney, J.J. and Sert, J.L. *Antonio Gaudí*.
  New York: Praeger Publishers, 1960.

PREFACE. How is a street or a vernacular architectural style assessed and why? The starting point of such a critical elaboration is the perception of the street and its adjacent buildings as the product of the historical process. It entails an analysis of all previous architecture and community building, both urban and rural, insofar as they have left remnants in popular construction methods. Inasmuch as vernacular architecture is largely the product of people to whom it never occurs that their history might have some possible importance and that there might be some value in leaving documentary evidence for it, our streets contain an infinity of historical traces without an inventory.

PART 1-- STORY OF THE ROAD.
ITALY. AN ANCIENT PATH.

A dry, frosty January day with a grey and rayless sky. The lake winds its way northwards between mountains that alternately advance upon and recede from a shoreline that is all gulfs and bays. There are clusters of lakeside development and on the mountainsides fields and scattered farms. The ancient path I was on was probably part of an ancient web of pathways that ran from settlement to settlement, mountain height to lakeside.

The ridgeways would be the oldest: the ground would have been more open, there would have been fewer trees to fell, and the well-drained soil would have provided the best road surface. However, as villages developed on

PATH

the more fertile land in the valleys,
roadways sufficiently above the valley floor
to provide decent drainage yet low enough
to avoid unnecessary climbing would have
been built. The main traffic would have
been diverted from hillcrest to hillside.

ROMAN ROAD. Sometimes the path ran level, sometimes steep. Occasionally it would narrow and plunge downward between walls of rock or come out onto a terrace of grass, pale brown and crushed beneath the winter sky. Not far from town it zigzagged down to a boggy area in which an earthen bank about fifteen feet wide, four to six feet high extended in a straight line about a mile in one direction and three in the other -- a remnant, perhaps, of a Roman road. If so, this mound might well conceal some ten feet of elaborate engineering: wood piles and beams, broken stone, finely beaten flint, stone slabs mixed with fine gravel.

ROAD IN TIMGAD (ALGERIA)

MILAN. The route to S. Ambrogio led diagonally across the bleak piazza. The cathedral front, blinking in the reflected light of advertisements, appeared to be an endless parade of posturing figures,

towers, and pinnacles -- affected,
devoid of energy and conviction.

The cold night air was damp and
penetrating. The vast piazza gave
way to a dimly lit maze of narrow,
twisting streets flanked by high
masonry walls, broken every now
and then with a shuttered window or
gaping archway. Echoing footsteps
were the only sounds.

At the time construction of the
gothic cathedral was started an
open sewer most likely ran down
the middle of these narrow, twisting
roadways, dividing them into even
more tortuous lanes that would be covered
with dust or mud according to the season.
Here and there heaps of dirty straw, the

219

beds of wretched beggars would have been trampled and mixed with the refuse on the roadways.

Suddenly ahead the floodlit bell tower of S. Ambrogio glowed warmly against the night sky. Drawing closer, the modest brick walls of the church could be seen, then a peaceful courtyard and in it a portico designed by Bramante.

The classical details of Bramante's design appeared soft, understated, and vibrating with energy. An occasional column shaft was carved in the representation of a tree trunk with the stubs of branches. The foliage of the capitals varied. The particular rationality of the Renaissance could be sensed. The darkness of the night seemed to stir, to widen.

Bramante knew the gothic alternative. He had recommended that the design of the unfinished portions of the cathedral conform to the existing structure. Yet, he turned his back on it and on the twisted roadways of Milan.

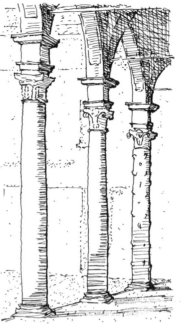

MILAN: Sant' Ambrogio, Porta della Canonica.

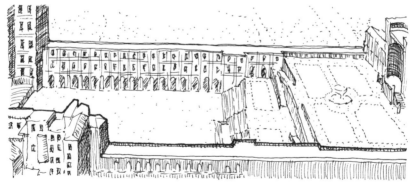

ROME: Bramante's design for the Belvedere Court, Vatican.

221

STARTING IN THE RENAISSANCE of the
fifteenth century -- wherever the capitalist
mode of production was developing within
the framework of feudalism, a new
flexibility in technological activities began to
emerge. The social distinction between
intellectual and physical work which had
developed under slavery began to break
down. Scholars discovered that the
practical knowledge and methods of
artisans could be of help in their
theoretical investigations, while artisans
learned that theoretical speculation could
be of help in their practical work.

The roads that meandered from city to
city in the fifteenth century were much the
same as they had been and would continue
to be for three hundred years: unpaved,
their outlines barely perceptible, recognizable
as roads only by the movement of those
making use of them -- peasants on foot,

someone leading an animal by its halter, a herdsman, a cart taking a farmer and his goods to market, occasionally a dashing horseman or a wheeled vehicle drawn by well-groomed horses. But a change had recently been made in such a vehicle-- its front carriage was now movable. This development marked the beginning of a steady increase of wheeled traffic which would make the earthen road totally inadequate by the end of the seventeenth century.

flat stone slabs
curbstone
broken tiles or bricks
compact rubble
stone blocks
subsoil
road raised above ground level
drainage ditch

ROMAN ROAD

stone chips and gravel
broken stone
stone blocks
subsoil
road level with ground

EIGHTEENTH-CENTURY ROAD

ground stones and stone powder
compacted 1" stones
subsoil
entire road construction arched

MACADAM ROAD

THE RAILWAY TRANSFORMED the concept of speed -- that is, the relation between time and space -- into something immeasurable by earlier standards. It revealed the possibilities of technical progress as nothing else had ever done: its use of novel and science-based technology (such as the electric telegraph) was unprecedented; its organization and methods unparalleled (the railway time-table became a symbol of exact, complex routine interlocked on a nation-wide basis that still fascinated Mussolini a hundred years after it was introduced). The sheer size and scale of the railway must have staggered the imagination (William Turner was not the only artist haunted by the image of Rain, Steam, and Speed). It dwarfed the most gigantic public works of the past.

This revolutionary transformation represented something more than the needs of an industrializing economy for transport. Like

1846

RAILWAY

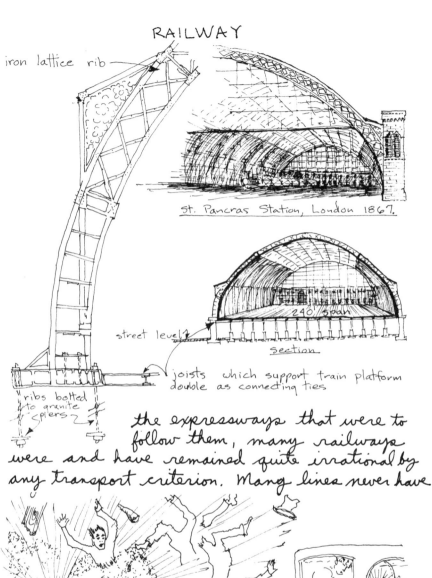

iron lattice rib

St. Pancras Station, London 1867.

240' span

street level

Section

joists which support train platform double as connecting ties

ribs bolted to granite piers

the expressways that were to follow them, many railways were and have remained quite irrational by any transport criterion. Many lines never have

After a drawing "Pleasures of the Railroad," 1831.

made more than the most modest profits, if they have made any at all. Most of England, where the railway was first developed, was within easy access of the sea, and water-transport was (and still is) the cheapest means of moving non-perishable bulk goods. However, there were people with money to invest, there were those who saw that there was money to be made in planning and building railways, if not in running them, and there was the romantic appeal of Progress.

MILAN: Galleria Vittorio Emanuele (1867).

MILAN. THE GALLERIA. It was in an arcade such as this that gas lighting was first used, but these "gas" fixtures are simulated -- as are the "tile" floors, the "marble" tables in the restaurants, and, worst of all, the "regional" food. In a way this peeling veneer of nineteenth-century opulence is an appropriate commentary, for the arcade was the invention of sales people, the creation of the newly industrialized luxury goods trade of the nineteenth century.

227

THE STREETS OF NEW YORK. Sparks and the screech of metal against asphalt paving. The wheel of a taxicab breaks loose and rolls wildly through a busy intersection of streets adjacent to Lincoln Center.

Splashing water. People lounge around the broad rim of the plaza fountain. A fashionably dressed couple promenade slowly across radiating lines of travertine paving.

Ballet at the Met: lights, color, music -- endless, effortless movement -- everything under control. The performance ends. People come down the thickly carpeted grand stair.

A siren screams on Ninth Avenue. An ambulance pulls up to the curb. Someone is placed on a stretcher. The ambulance starts off. Its siren blends into the wail of the street.

The promenading couple return to the box office to buy tickets for the next performance.

NEW YORK CITY: Lincoln Center for the Performing Arts (1962-68).

228

PART 2 -- CITY STREETS.

MONTREAL, 1976. The Olympic Games Organizing Committee had been given a $386,000 grant from the Quebec provincial government to put on an arts exhibition and festival that would run concurrently with the Summer Olympics. The site chosen for the exhibition was a 5½-mile stretch of Sherbrooke Street, a street that was to be the main access to the Olympics compound, but also a street that contained much of the city's history: Montreal's oldest residences, local businesses, religious and educational buildings; newest office buildings, chain stores, and fast food places; and an increasing number of empty lots that represented a development program, sponsored by the mayor, whose goal seemed to be to replace as much of the old streetscape with as much of the new as possible.

NORTHAMPTON, MASS: View of Main Street from newer commercial strip. The architectural details presented in this essay are all on or near Main Street unless noted otherwise.

The exhibition, in which 75 architects, artists, and designers participated, was intended to show Sherbrooke Street as a collective art work. The facades of the demolished buildings were recreated in plywood in the empty lots, huge photographs of their handcrafted details were mounted on scaffolding, banners were designed, maps and murals painted, street sculpture erected. It was called Corridart and was officially opened on July 7. The mayor refused to attend, but not the news media, which gave the event extensive coverage.

On the evening of July 13 the mayor acted. He sent 75 municipal employees and more than 20 trucks, bulldozers, cherry pickers, and cranes to Sherbrooke Street. By morning Corridart had been utterly destroyed. The mayor's people smashed and carried off the $386,000 worth of sculpture, banners, photographs, stages, benches, and scaffolding. The next day they razed the plywood facades that had recreated the earlier street. Everything was lugged to the municipal dump, much of it incinerated.

The creation of Corridart by 15 artists, designers, and architects was a political act. It viewed the city street as a historical document and collective work of art. It described the unity of life and art as active and critical, not passive and accepting.

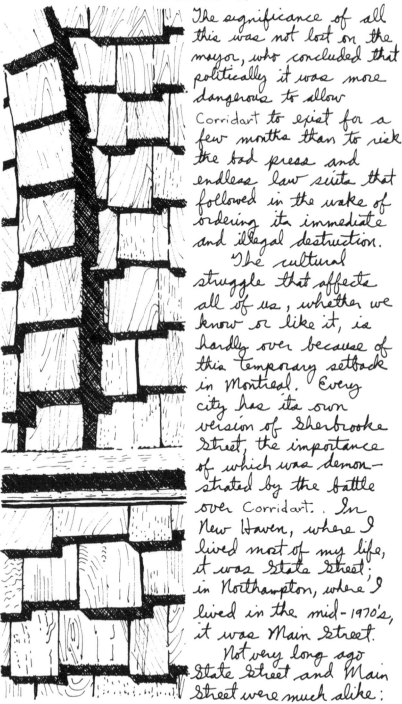

The significance of all this was not lost on the mayor, who concluded that politically it was more dangerous to allow Corridart to exist for a few months than to risk the bad press and endless law suits that followed in the wake of ordering its immediate and illegal destruction.

The cultural struggle that affects all of us, whether we know or like it, is hardly over because of this temporary setback in Montreal. Every city has its own version of Sherbrooke Street, the importance of which was demonstrated by the battle over Corridart. In New Haven, where I lived most of my life, it was State Street; in Northampton, where I lived in the mid-1970's, it was Main Street.

Not very long ago State Street and Main Street were much alike:

both were lined with old, masonry-surfaced buildings with small, not very active businesses on the ground floor. The three to five stories above were mostly vacant, their large, sometimes marvelously detailed windows broken or boarded up.

Since 1970 State Street has been a wasteland. The city administration cleared it in order to build a half-mile long, five-story high parking garage, in spite of the fact that the number of cars using the other garages that had been built was already seriously below the anticipated figure.

Main Street, on the other hand, began to thrive in the early 1970's. With impetus from the five colleges in the area that began to recognize Northampton as their urban center, new businesses moved into the vacant space on the ground floor: various kinds of restaurants, such as an ice cream parlor and soup and salad place; specialty shops, such as an organic foods outlet, craft galleries and suppliers, book and music stores.

above them, long unused space was turned into lofts and apartments: the owner of one building gave the top floor rent free for five years to a couple who rehabilitated it at their own expense -- putting in a new kitchen and bathroom, repairing the old chimneys for new wood burning heaters, uncovering brick walls, and refinishing the old woodwork.

Joan and I lived on the floor below in a large, two-story space with a ceiling of heavy wood beams and curved wood struts, the skeleton of what was probably a richly ornamented, vaulted plaster ceiling. Apparently, the space began as a fashionable ballroom, but more recently had been used for little more than dead storage for the offices below it and the shops on the ground floor.

Joan choreographs and performs solo dances stripped of theatricality. She had a studio in the last remaining warehouse on State Street. much of her art grew out of and related to the struggles of the people who lived and worked there. at one time the residents of a low-priced residential hotel scheduled for demolition banded together in protest. at a rally held in the hotel lobby Joan performed a dance about a person who might well have been one of them. It was titled, "When the landlord left I did the only thing a poor soul can do, I walked around the room and scratched my head." at the end of the

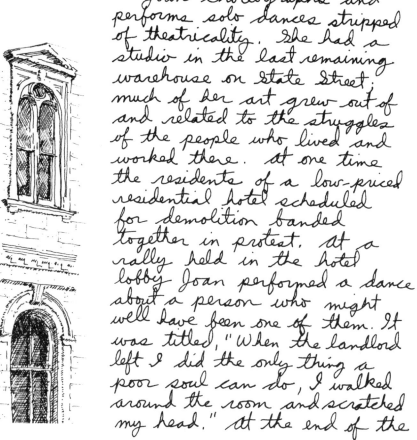

performance and discussion that followed, she was handed a note:

    I am glad that you came and showed us your play. Did you ever see the man they put out on the street? Was he old or young? Some people that I know got relocated. We don't want to be relocated.

    The foot taps you did were good and nobody can do them like you. My sister and I wanted to learn steps like that.

    Everyone was glad that you came. Will you come back again?

Unfortunately a second performance never took place. The hotel was demolished. The residents had to separate. A few of them died in the process of being relocated. The rest of them lost contact with the area. Joan, too, was forced to move.

236

PROJECT. FIREHOUSE ARTS CENTER.

"It seems that the City is about to sell the old Elm Street firehouse." He was an old friend and had telephoned to ask if I could meet with him immediately. He had placed his chair squarely in front of mine and was leaning forward, his hands placed firmly on his knees.

"There's a group of us. We have the money to buy the building at the price they're asking. We figure we can raise the additional amount to fix it up properly." He paused, then continued. "In the old days, in the 1930's, working people produced plays and exhibits; our own art, dance, and music; pageants about our struggle. We need a place to have those kinds of exchanges again."

"The firehouse is small for an arts center," I said, "but in a good location -- downtown, on the edge of the Dwight and Dixwell neighborhoods. But don't you think the whole deal is in some politician's pocket?"

"They've set it up as a competition," he answered. "We just heard about it, and

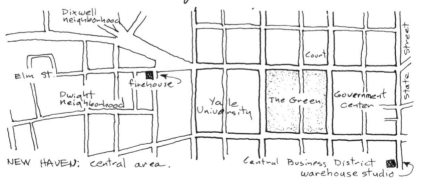

NEW HAVEN: central area.

237

PROJECT

the deadline is next week. We're supposed
to submit drawings and a financial statement."

The functional requirements of the
proposed arts facility would not be costly:
a new wood floor, some minor plumbing and
electrical work, a new stair and entrance.
The existing overhead door adjacent to
the street intersection would provide access
for deliveries and make an effective billboard.
The openings for the three other overhead
doors would be filled in with glass block
to the height of the 7'-0" doorway in the
center of the now asymmetrical elevation, which

PROJECT: design study.

would be filled entirely with glass block.
Clear glass would be installed between the
existing windows in the proposed gallery
space on the second floor and above the
sections of glass block in the overhead
door openings. The new windows on the
first floor would echo the slightly off-center
placement of the existing second floor windows,
and the new glass block entrance would
echo the design of the roof parapet.

"Firehouse Arts Center -- Yes!" Posters
taped onto utility poles and store windows
throughout the area announced a "living
petition" in support of the proposal.

The parking lot across the street from
the firehouse filled with people. Painters and
craftspeople carried examples of their work
like picket signs, a neighborhood chorus
and theater group performed, a jazz
group, folksingers, poets. Joan presented
a dance called "Growing." It ended with
the audience being drawn into an ever

tighter, whirling circle, then released -- a group formed, then dispersed.

A reporter, who happened upon the event by accident, wrote an article that was prominently placed on the back page of the next evening's newspaper.

In the next few weeks the competition was news. It was a feature story in the Sunday paper, on local TV and radio programs. The arts center proposal began to accumulate endorsements.

The politicians acted quickly. The firehouse was given to a prominent real estate firm that, according to the official announcement, "promised to turn it into a high-class restaurant."

The group that sang and danced together in the parking lot dispersed.

QUESTIONS

The demolition of State Street in New Haven and transformation of Sherbrooke Street in Montreal represented new programs of urban development that were being implemented amid various forms of protest, such as the "living petition" and "corridart." An ever increasing number of people were arguing that something was wrong with a development program that required a substantial and systematic obliteration of the past; something important was irretrievably lost in the process. Struggles that cut across "progressive" and "conservative" political lines attempted to stop the bulldozers; save this or that building, street, or park; and, in general, rethink the political proposition that new is always better than old. The rehabilitation of Main Street in Northampton seemed to represent an alternative to the total transformation of an existing street, but there were questions that applied equally well to both forms of development:

MILAN: cityscape.

241

QUESTIONS

What groups of people were participating in and benefiting from the particular form the development was taking? What groups were not? In comparison with State Street, the development of Main Street involved more developers using less money and a more modest building technology, but neither form of development addressed the problems of those with little or no access to money or power. Different but related economic interests were responsible for the large-scale demolition of State Street and small-scale rehabilitation of Main Street.

A contrary notion about the significance of the buildings that collectively form a major downtown street was dramatized by the creation of "corridart" and, in a more modest way, by the "living petition" in support of the Firehouse Arts Center. What precisely were these two groups of architects and artists trying to say?

A street together with the buildings on either side of it forms a distinct cultural idea. The architecture of a street is not this or that style, designs of this or that architect, or even this or that broad section of popular building types. It is a process that combines all of these elements and culminates in an overall trend. It is contained in the tools, materials, and building notions common to the place and time in which

the street is built -- and in the way the builders of the street see things and act. The architecture of a street is a history of that street as that history is given concrete shape and substance. In short, it would be a mistake to think of vernacular architecture as something independent of and opposed to the concept of history articulated by architects.

An architect identifies with a particular group of people who share a mode of thinking and acting. Each architect is one-of-many, that is, a collective person. Creating a new architectural statement entails more than the articulation of original discoveries. It also, and more particularly, entails the concretizing and diffusion of all that has been discovered previously about a particular set of building problems. Architecture does not exist on its own, in and for itself. It is not an individual and socially isolated activity. It is a part of a cultural struggle to transform the way people see the world and act.

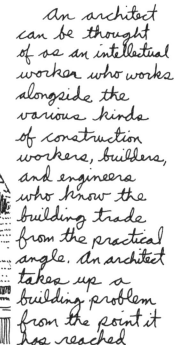

An architect can be thought of as an intellectual worker who works alongside the various kinds of construction workers, builders, and engineers who know the building trade from the practical angle. An architect takes up a building problem from the point it has reached after it has undergone every previous attempt at a solution -- that is, besides the practical aspects of the problem, an architect is concerned with its theoretical and historical aspects as well.

The creation of "corridart" in Montreal, the effort to convert an old firehouse into a community arts center in New Haven, the insertion of a classical portico into the medieval street pattern of Milan are three randomly chosen examples of how the work of architects is molded by the active relationship which exists between them and the cultural environment they are proposing to change.

All three examples presuppose a shared concept of the street and its buildings that is clear and strong enough to weld together a multiplicity of dispersed wills with heterogeneous aims. Such a moment of cultural unity is important, for no matter how briefly it may echo through the streets of a particular community, it produces a cultural climate inspiring to others. It is as valuable as it is vulnerable to the bulldozers of those people who wish to treat the street as if it were their personal property.

246

RESPONSE

Sherbrooke, State, Main, many streets are important not because they represent some imaginary golden age in the past or because they are an exploitable economic resource in the present, but because they indicate the path of history, the direction of its development -- the future that is within our grasp if we understand that we must reach out and claim it.

SOURCES (in order of appearance in essay)

Gregory, J.W. The Story of the Road. London: Black Ltd., 1938.

Wittkower, Rudolf. Gothic Vs. Classic. New York: Braziller, 1974.

Lilley, Samuel. Men, Machines, and History. New York: International Publishers, 1965.

Hobsbawm, E.J. Industry and Empire. Harmondsworth, Middlesex: Penguin Books Ltd., 1969.

Kuhn, Annette. "The Rape of Sherbrooke," Village Voice (New York), August 2, 1976.

MacDonald, William. Northampton, Massachusetts. Northampton: Northampton Bicentennial Committee, 1975.

Gramsci, Antonio. Selections from the Prison Notebooks. New York: International Publishers, 1971.

"An Interview with E.P. Thompson," Radical History Review 3, No. 4 (Fall 1976): 4-25.